PEACE & HOLINESS

Horatius Bonar

PEACE & HOLINESS

WARHORN
MEDIA

Peace & Holiness

Warhorn Media
2401 S. Endwright Rd.
Bloomington, IN 47403
WarhornMedia.com

God's Way of Peace originally published 1861. *God's Way of Holiness* originally published 1864. This combined edition published 2017. Public Domain.

Cover design by Ben Crum
Interior layout by Alex McNeilly. Typeset in 11/14 pt. Adobe Garamond Pro.

Printed in the United States of America
21 20 19 18 17   1 2 3 4 5

ISBN-13: 978-1-940017-12-9 (paperback)
ISBN-13: 978-1-940017-13-6 (EPUB)
ISBN-13: 978-1-940017-14-3 (Mobi/Kindle)

Contents

GOD'S WAY OF PEACE

Preface 3
1. God's Testimony Concerning Man 7
2. Man's Own Character No Ground for Peace 11
3. God's Character Our Resting Place 19
4. Righteous Grace 27
5. The Blood of Sprinkling 33
6. The Person and Work of the Substitute 39
7. The Word of the Truth of the Gospel 47
8. Believe and Be Saved 57
9. Believe Just Now 65
10. The Want of Power to Believe 73
11. Insensibility 83
12. Jesus Only 91

GOD'S WAY OF HOLINESS

Preface 109
1. The New Life 111
2. Christ for Us, the Spirit in Us 125

3. The Root and Soil of Holiness. 137
4. Strength against Sin. 151
5. The Cross and Its Power. 159
6. The Saint and the Law 171
7. The Saint and the Seventh Chapter of Romans 189
8. The True Creed and the True Life 199
9. Counsels and Warnings. 211

God's Way of
PEACE

Preface

There seem to be many, in our day, who are seeking God. Yet they appear to be but "feeling after Him, in order to find Him," as if He were either a distant or an "unknown" God. They forget that he is "not far from every one of us" (Acts 17:27); for "in him we live, and move, and have our being."

That He is not far; that He has come down; that He has come near—this is the "beginning of the gospel." It sets aside the vain thoughts of those who think that they must bring Him near by their prayers and devout performances. He has shown Himself to us, that we may know Him, and, in knowing Him, find the life of our souls.

With some who call themselves Christians, religion is a very unfinished thing. It drags heavily, and is not satisfactory, either to the religious performers of it, or the onlookers. There is no substance in it, and no comfort. There is earnestness perhaps, but there is no "peace with God"; and so there is not even the root or foundation of that which God calls "religion." It needs to begin over again.

Acceptance with God lies at the foundation of all religion, for there must be an accepted worshipper before there can be acceptable worship. Religion is, with many, merely the means of averting God's displeasure and securing His favour. It is often irksome, but they do not feel easy in neglecting it; and they hope that by it they may obtain forgiveness before they die.

This, however, is the inversion of God's order, and is in reality the worship of an unknown God. It terminates in forgiveness, whereas God's religion begins with it. All false religions, though outwardly differing very widely, are made up of earnest efforts to secure for the religionists the divine favour now, and eternal life at last. The one true religion is seen in the holy life of those who, having found for themselves forgiveness and favour, in believing the record which God has given of His Son, are walking with Him from day to day, in the calm but sure consciousness of being entirely accepted, and working for Him, with the happy earnestness of those whose reward is His constant smile of love; who, having been much forgiven, love much, and show, by daily sacrifice and service, how much they feel themselves debtors to a redeeming God, debtors to His church, and debtors to the world in which they live (Rom 1:14).

But if this is true religion, how much is there of the false?

It is not good that men should be all their life seeking God, and never finding Him; that they should be ever learning, and never able to come to the knowledge of the truth. It is not good to be always doubting; and, when challenged, to make the untrue excuse that they are only doubting themselves, not God; that they are only dissatisfied with their own faith, but not with its glorious object. It is not good to believe in our own faith, still less in our own doubts, as some seem to do, making the best doubter to be the best believer; as if it were the gold of the cup, not the living water which it contains, that was to quench our thirst; and as if it were unlawful to take that precious water from a poor earthen vessel, such as our imperfect faith must ever be! In this momentous thing, surely it is with the water, and not with the vessel, that the thirsty soul has to do! It is not the quality of the vessel, but the quality of the water, that the thirsty soul thinks of; and he whose pride will not allow him to drink out of a soiled or broken pitcher must die of thirst. So he who puts away the sure reconciliation of the cross, because of an imperfect faith, must die the death. He who says, "I believe the right thing, but I don't believe it in the right way, and therefore I can't have peace," is the man whose pride is such, that he is determined not to quench his thirst save out of a cup of gold.

Some have tried to give directions to sinners "how to get converted," multiplying words without wisdom, leading the sinner away from the cross by setting him upon *doing*, not upon *believing*. Our business is not to give any such directions, but, as the apostles did, to preach Christ crucified, a present Saviour, and a present salvation. Then it is that sinners are converted, as the Lord Himself said, "I, if I be lifted up . . . will draw all men unto me" (Jn 12:32).

In the following chapters there are some things which may appear repetitions. But this could not easily be avoided, as there were certain truths as well as certain errors that necessarily came up at different points and under different aspects. I need not apologise for these, as they were, in a great measure, unavoidable. They take up very little space, and I do not think they will seem at all superfluous to anyone who reads for profit and not for criticism.

Horatius Bonar
Kelso, Scotland
December 1861

I

God's Testimony Concerning Man

God knows us. He knows what we are; He knows also what He meant us to be; and, upon the difference between these two states, He founds His testimony concerning us.

He is too loving to say anything needlessly severe; too true to say anything untrue; nor can He have any motive to misrepresent us; for He loves to tell of the good, not of the evil, that may be found in any of the works of His hands. He declared them good, "very good," at first; and if He does not do so now, it is not because He would not, but because He cannot; for "all flesh has corrupted its way upon the earth" (Gn 6:12).

The divine testimony concerning man is that he is a sinner. God bears witness against him, not for him; and testifies that "there is none righteous, no, not one"; that there is "none that doeth good"; none "that understandeth"; none that even seeks after God, and, still more, none that loves Him (Ps 14:1–3; Rom

3:10–12). God speaks of man kindly, but severely; as one yearning over a lost child, yet as one who will make no terms with sin, and will "by no means clear the guilty." He declares man to be a lost one, a stray one, a rebel, a "hater of God" (Rom 1:30); not a sinner occasionally, but a sinner always; not a sinner in part, with many good things about him; but wholly a sinner, with no compensating goodness; evil in heart as well as life, "dead in trespasses and sins" (Eph 2:1); an evil doer, and therefore under condemnation; an enemy of God, and therefore "under wrath"; a breaker of the righteous law, and therefore under "the curse of the law" (Gal 3:10).

Man has fallen! Not this man nor that man, but the whole race. In Adam all have sinned; in Adam all have died. It is not that a few leaves have faded or been shaken down, but the tree has become corrupt, root and branch. The "flesh," or "old man"—that is, each man as he is born into the world, a son of man, a fragment of humanity, a unit in Adam's fallen body—is "corrupt." The sinner not merely brings forth sin, but he carries it about with him, as his second self; he is a "body" or mass of sin (Rom 6:6), a "body of death" (Rom 7:24), subject not to the law of God, but to "the law of sin" (Rom 7:23). The Jew, educated under the most perfect of laws, and in the most favourable circumstances, was the best type of humanity, of civilised, polished, educated humanity; the best specimen of Adam's sons; yet God's testimony concerning him is that he is "under sin," that he has gone astray, and that he has "come short of the glory of God."

The outer life of a man is not the man, just as the paint on a piece of timber is not the timber, and as the green moss upon the hard rock is not the rock itself. The picture of a man is not the man; it is but a skillful arrangement of colours which look like the man. So it is the bearing of the soul toward God that is the true state of the man. The man that loves God with all his heart is in a right state; the man that does not love Him thus is in a wrong one. He is a sinner, because his heart is not right with

God. He may think his life a good one, and others may think the same; but God counts him guilty, worthy of death and hell. The outward good cannot make up for the inward evil. The good deeds done to his fellow men cannot be set off against his bad thoughts of God. And he must be full of these bad thoughts, so long as he does not love this infinitely lovable and infinitely glorious Being with all his strength.

God's testimony then concerning man is that he does not love God with all his heart; indeed, that he does not love Him at all. Not to love our neighbour is sin; not to love a parent is greater sin; but not to love God is greater sin still.

Man need not try to say a good word for himself, or to plead "not guilty," unless he can show that he loves, and has always loved God with his whole heart and soul. If he can truly say this, he is all right, he is not a sinner, and does not need pardon. He will find his way to the kingdom without the cross and without a Saviour. But, if he cannot say this, "his mouth is stopped," and he is "guilty before God." However favourably a good outward life may dispose him and others to look upon his case just now, the verdict will go against him hereafter. This is man's day, when man's judgments prevail; but God's day is coming, when the case shall be tried upon its real merits. Then the Judge of all the earth shall do right, and the sinner be put to shame.

There is another and yet worse charge against him. He does not believe on the name of the Son of God, nor love the Christ of God. This is his sin of sins. That his heart is not right with God is the first charge against him. That his heart is not right with the Son of God is the second. And it is this second that is the crowning, crushing sin, carrying with it more terrible damnation than all other sins together. "He that believeth not is condemned already, because he hath not believed in the name of the only begotten Son of God" (Jn 3:18). "He that believeth not God hath made him a liar; because he believeth not the record that God gave of his Son" (1 Jn 5:10). "He that believeth not shall be damned" (Mk 16:16). And hence it is that the first sin which the Holy Spirit brings home to a man is unbelief; "when he [the Holy Spirit] is come, he will reprove the world of sin . . . because they believe not on me" (Jn 16:8–9).

Such is God's condemnation of man. Of this the whole Bible is full. That great love of God, which His Word reveals, is based on this condemnation. It is love to the condemned. God's testimony to His own grace has no meaning, save as resting on, or taking for granted His testimony to man's guilt and ruin. Nor is it against man as merely a being morally diseased or sadly unfortunate that He testifies, but as guilty of death, under wrath, sentenced to the eternal curse, for that crime of crimes, a heart not right with God, and not true to His incarnate Son.

This is a divine verdict, not a human one. It is God, not man, who condemns, and God is not a man that He should lie. This is God's testimony concerning man, and we know that this witness is true. It concerns us much to receive it as such, and act upon it.

2

Man's Own Character No Ground for Peace

If God testifies against us, who can testify for us? If God's opinion of man's sinfulness, His judgment of man's guilt, and His declaration of sin's evil, is so very decided, there can be no hope of acquittal for us on the ground of personal character or goodness, either of heart or life. That which God sees in us furnishes only matter for condemnation, not for pardon.

It is vain to struggle or murmur against God's judgment. He is the Judge of all the earth; and He is right as well as sovereign in His judgment. He must be obeyed; His law is inexorable; it cannot be broken without making the breaker of it (even in one jot or tittle) worthy of death.

When the Holy Spirit opens the eyes of the soul, it sees this. Conviction of sin is just the sinner seeing himself as he is, and as God has all along seen him. Then every fond idea of self-goodness, either in whole or in part, vanishes away. The things in him that once seemed good appear so bad, and the bad things so very bad, that every self-prop falls from beneath him, and all hope of being saved, in consequence of something in his own character, is then taken away. He sees that he cannot save himself; nor help God to save him. He is lost, and he is helpless. Doings, feelings, strivings, prayings, givings, abstainings, and the like, are found to be no relief from a sense of guilt, and, therefore, no resting place for a troubled heart. If sin were but a disease or a misfortune, these apparent good things might relieve him, as being favourable symptoms of returning health; but when sin is guilt even more than disease; and when the sinner is not merely sick, but condemned by the righteous Judge, then none of these goodnesses, whether inner or outer, can reach his case, for they cannot assure him of a complete and righteous pardon, and, therefore, cannot pacify his roused and wounded conscience. He sees God's unchangeable hatred of sin, and the coming revelation of His wrath against the sinner; and he cannot but tremble.

The question, "Wherewith shall I come before the Lord?" is not one which can be decided by an appeal to personal character or goodness of life, or prayers, or performances of religion. The way of approach is not for us to settle. God has settled it; and it only remains for us to avail ourselves of it. He has fixed it on grounds altogether irrespective of our character; or rather on grounds which take for granted simply that we are sinners, and that therefore the element of goodness in us, as a title, or warrant, or recommendation, is altogether inadmissible, either in whole or in part.

Man is bankrupt, totally so; his credit in the market is gone. If, then, he is to carry on his trade, he cannot do it in his own name. He must have a better name than that, a name of note and weight, for his security. For the transactions of the heavenly market there is but one name given under heaven, the Name of names.

To say, as some do at the outset of their anxiety, "I will set myself to pray, and after I have prayed a sufficient length of time, and with tolerable earnestness, I may approach and count upon acceptance," is not only to build upon the quality and quantity of our prayers, but it is to overlook the real question before the sinner, "How am I to approach God in order to pray?" All prayers are approaches to God, and the sinner's anxious question is, "How may I approach God?" God's explicit testimony to man is, "You are unfit to approach me"; and it is a denial of the testimony to say, "I will pray myself out of this unfitness into fitness; I will work myself into a right state of mind and character for drawing near to God."

Were you from this moment to cease from sin, and do nothing but good all the rest of your life, it would be of no avail. Were you to begin praying now, and do nothing else but pray all your days, it would not do. Your own character cannot be your way of approach, nor your ground of confidence toward God. No amount of praying, or working, or feeling, can satisfy the righteous law, or pacify a guilty conscience, or quench the flaming sword that guards the access into the presence of the infinitely Holy One.

That which makes it safe for you to draw near to God, and right for God to receive you, must be something altogether away from and independent of yourself; for God has already condemned yourself and everything pertaining to yourself; and no condemned thing can give you any warrant for going to Him, or hoping for acceptance. Your liberty of entrance must come from something which He has accepted, not from something which He has condemned.

I knew an awakened soul who, in the bitterness of his spirit, thus set himself to work and pray, in order to get peace. He doubled the amount of his devotions, saying to himself, "Surely God will give me peace." But the peace did not come. He set up family worship, saying, "Surely God will give me peace."

Again the peace did not come. At last he thought of having a prayer meeting in his house, as a certain remedy; he fixed the night, called his neighbours, and prepared himself for conducting the meeting by writing a prayer and learning it by heart. As he finished the operation of learning it, preparatory to the meeting, he threw it down on the table saying, "Surely that will do; God will give me peace now." In that moment a still small voice seemed to speak in his ear, saying, "No, that will not do; but Christ will do." Straightaway the scales fell from his eyes, and the burden from his shoulders. Peace poured in like a river. "Christ will do," was his watchword ever after.

Very clear is God's testimony against man, and man's doings, in this great matter of approach and acceptance. "Not by works of righteousness which we have done," says Paul in one place (Ti 3:5); "to him that worketh not," says he in a second (Rom 4:5); "not justified by the works of the law" says he in a third (Gal 2:16).

The sinner's peace with God is not to come from his own character. No grounds of peace or elements of reconciliation can be extracted from himself, either directly or indirectly. His one qualification for peace is that he needs it. It is not what he has but what he lacks of good that draws him to God; and it is the consciousness of this lack that bids him look elsewhere, for something both to invite and embolden him to approach. It is our sickness, not our health, that fits us for the physician, and casts us upon his skill.

No guilty conscience can be pacified with anything short of that which will make pardon a present, a sure, and a righteous thing. Can our best doings, our best feelings, our best prayers, our best sacrifices, bring this about? No! Having accumulated these to the utmost, the sinner feels that pardon is just as far off and uncertain as before; and that all his earnestness cannot persuade God to admit him to favour, or bribe his own conscience into true quiet even for an hour.

In all false religion, the worshipper rests his hope of divine favour upon something in his own character, or life, or religious duties. The Pharisee did this when he came into the temple, thanking God that he was "not as other men" (Lk 18:11). So do those in our day who expect to get peace by doing, feeling, and praying more than others, or than they themselves have done in time past; and who refuse to take the peace of the free gospel, till they have amassed such an amount of doing and feeling as will ease their consciences, and make them conclude that it would not be fair in God to reject the application of men so earnest and devoted as they.

The Galatians did this also when they insisted on adding the law of Moses to the gospel of Christ, as the ground of confidence toward God. Thus do many act among ourselves. They will not take confidence from God's character or Christ's work but from their own character and work; though in reference to all this it is written, "The Lord hath rejected thy confidences, and thou shalt not prosper in them" (Jer 2:37). They object to a present confidence, for that assumes that a sinner's resting place is wholly outside himself—ready made, as it were, by God. They would have this confidence to be a very gradual thing, in order that they may gain time, and, by a little diligence in religious observances, so add to their stock of duties, prayers, experiences, devotions, that they may, with some "humble hope"—as they call it—claim acceptance from God. By this course of devout living they think they have made themselves more acceptable to God than they were before they began this religious process, and much more entitled to expect the divine favour than those who have not so qualified themselves. In all this, the attempted resting place is self, that self which God has condemned. They would not rest upon unpraying, or unworking, or undevout self; but they think it right and safe to rest upon praying, and working, and devout self—and they call this humility! The happy confidence of the simple believer who takes God's Word at once, and rests on it, they call presumption or fanaticism; their own miserable uncertainty, extracted from the doings of self, they speak of as a humble hope.

The sinner's own character, in any form, and under any process of improvement, cannot furnish reasons for trusting God. However amended, it cannot speak peace to his conscience, nor afford him any warrant for reckoning on God's favour; nor can it help to heal the breach between him and God. For God can accept nothing but perfection in such a case, and the sinner has nothing but imperfection to present. Imperfect duties and devotions cannot persuade God to forgive.

Besides, be it remembered that the person of the worshipper must be accepted before his services can be acceptable; so that nothing can be of any use to the sinner, save that which provides for personal acceptance completely, and at the outset. The sinner must go to God as he is, or not at all. To try to pray himself into something better than a condemned sinner, in order to win God's favour, is to make prayer an instrument of self-righteousness; so that, instead of its being the act of an accepted man, it is the price of acceptance, the money which we pay to God for favouring us, and the bribe with which we persuade conscience no longer to trouble us with its terrors.

No knowledge of self, nor consciousness of improvement of self, can soothe the alarms of an awakened conscience, or be any ground for expecting the friendship of God. To take comfort from our good doings, or good feelings, or good intentions, or good prayers, or good experiences, is to delude ourselves, and to say peace when there is no peace. No man can find rest from his own character, however good; or from his own acts, however religious. Even were he perfect, what enjoyment could there be in thinking about his own perfection? What profit, then, or what peace, can there be in thinking about his own *im*perfection?

Even were there many good things about him, they could not speak peace; for the good things which might speak peace could not make up for the evil things which speak trouble; and what a poor, self-made peace would that be which arose from his thinking as much good and as little evil of himself as possible! And what a temptation, besides, would this furnish to extenuate the evil and exaggerate the good about ourselves; in other words, to deceive our own hearts. Self-deception must always, more or less, be the result of such estimates of our own experiences. Laid open, as we are, in such a case, to all manner of self-blinding influences, it is impossible that we can be impartial judges, as in the case of those who are freely and at once forgiven.

One man might say, "My sins are not very great or many; surely I may have peace." Another might say, "I have made up for my sins by my good deeds; I may have peace." Another might say, "I have a very deep sense of sin; I may have peace." Another might say, "I have repented of my sin; I may have peace." Another might say, "I pray much; I work much; I love much; I give much; I may have peace." What temptation in all this to take the most favourable view of self and its doings! But, after all, it would be vain. There could be no real peace; for the foundation would be sand, not rock. The peace and confidence which come from summing up the good points of our character, or thinking of our good feelings and doings, or setting a certain valuation upon our faith, and love, and repentance, must be made up of pride. Its basis is self-righteousness, or, at least, self-approbation.

It does not mend the matter to say that we look at these good feelings in us as the Spirit's work, not our own. In one aspect this takes away boasting, but in another it does not. It still makes our peace to turn upon what is in ourselves, and not on what is in God. In fact, it makes use of the Holy Spirit for purposes of self-righteousness. It says that the Spirit works the change in us, in order that He may thereby furnish us with a ground of peace within ourselves.

No doubt the Spirit's work in us must be accompanied with peace, but not because He has given us something in ourselves from which to draw our peace. It is that kind of peace which arises unconsciously from the restoration of spiritual health, but not that which Scripture calls "peace with God." It does not arise from thinking about the change wrought in us, but unconsciously and involuntarily from the change itself. If a broken limb be made whole, we get relief straight away—not by thinking about the healed member, but simply in the bodily ease and comfort which the cure has given. So there is a peace arising out of the change of nature and character wrought by the Spirit, but this is not reconciliation with God. This is not the peace which the knowledge of forgiveness brings. It accompanies it, and flows from it, but the two kinds of peace are quite distinct from each other. Nor does even the peace which attends the restoration of spiritual health come secondhand, from thinking about our change; but directly from the change itself. That change is the soul's new health, and this health is in itself a continual gladness.

It remains true, then, that in ourselves we have no resting place. It is the quality of the work without, not the quality of that within, which satisfies us. "No confidence in the flesh" must be our motto, as it is the foundation of God's gospel.

3

God's Character Our Resting Place

We have seen that a sinner's peace cannot come from himself, nor from the knowledge of himself, nor from thinking about his own acts and feelings, nor from believing in his own faith, nor from the consciousness of any amendment of his old self.

Whence, then, is it to come? How does he get it?

It can only come from God; and it is in knowing God that he gets it. God has written a Volume for the purpose of making Himself known; and it is in this revelation of His character that the sinner is to find the rest that he is seeking. God Himself is the fountainhead of our peace; His revealed truth is the channel through which this peace finds its way to us; and His Holy Spirit is the great Interpreter of that truth to us. "Acquaint now thyself with him [God], and be at peace" (Job 22:21). Yes; acquaintanceship with God is peace!

Had God told us that He was not gracious, that He took no interest in our welfare, and that He had no intention of pardoning us, we could have had no peace and no hope. In that case our knowing God would only make us miserable. Our situation would be like that of the devils, who "believe, and tremble" (Jas 2:19); and the more that we knew of such a God, we should tremble the more. For how fearful a thing must it be to have the great God that made us, the great Father of spirits, against us, not for us!

Strange to say, this is the very state of disquietude in which we find many who yet profess to believe in a God "merciful and gracious"! With the Bible in their hands, and the cross before their eyes, they wander on in a state of darkness and fear, just such as would have arisen had God revealed himself in hatred, not in love. They seem to believe the very opposite of what the Bible teaches us concerning God; and to attach a meaning to the cross the reverse of what the gospel affirms it really bears. Had God been all frowns, and the Bible all terrors, and Christ all sternness, these men could not have been in a more troubled and uncertain state than that in which they are.

How is this? Have they not misunderstood the Bible? Have they not mistaken the character of God, looking on Him as an "austere man" and a "hard master"? Are they not labouring to supplement the grace of God by something on their part, as if they believed that this grace was not sufficient to meet their case, until they had attracted it to themselves by some earnest performances, or gloomy experiences, or alarming convictions, or spiritual exercises, of their own?

God has declared Himself to be gracious. "God is love." He has embodied this grace in the person and work of His beloved Son. He has told us that this grace is for the ungodly, the unholy, the rebellious, the dead in sin. The more, then, that we know of this God and of His grace, the more will His peace fill us. Nor will the greatness of our sins, and the hardness of our hearts, or the changeableness of our feelings, discourage or disquiet, however much they may humble us, and make us dissatisfied with ourselves.

Let us study the character of God: holy, yet loving; the love not interfering with the holiness, nor the holiness with the love; absolutely sovereign, yet infinitely gracious—the sovereignty not limiting the grace, nor grace relaxing the sovereignty; drawing the unwilling, yet not hindering the willing, if any such there be; quickening whom He will, yet having no pleasure in the death of the wicked; compelling some to come in, yet freely inviting all! Let us look at Him in the face of Jesus Christ, for He is the express image of His person, and he that has seen Him has seen the Father. The knowledge of that gracious character, as interpreted by the cross of Christ, is the true remedy for our disquietudes.

Insufficient acquaintanceship with God lies at the root of our fears and gloom. I know that flesh and blood cannot reveal God to you, and that the Holy Spirit alone can enable you to know either the Father or the Son. But I would not have you for a moment suppose that the Spirit is reluctant to do His work in you; nor would I encourage you in the awful thought that you are willing, while He is unwilling; or that the sovereignty of God is a hindrance to the sinner, and a restraint of the Spirit. The whole Bible takes for granted that all this is absolutely impossible. Never can the great truths of divine sovereignty and the Spirit's work land us, as some seem to think they may do, in such a conflict between a willing sinner and an unwilling God.

The whole Bible is so written by the Spirit, and the gospel was so preached by the apostles, as never to raise the question of God's willingness, nor to lead to the remotest suspicion of His readiness to furnish the sinner with all needed aid. Hence the great truths of God's eternal election, and Christ's redemption of His Church, as we read them in the Bible, are helps and encouragements to the soul. But, interpreted as they are by many, they seem barrier walls, not ladders for scaling the great barrier walls of man's unwillingness; and anxious souls become landlocked in metaphysical questions and self-righteous perplexities, out of which there can be no way of extrication, save that of taking God at His word.

In the Bible God has revealed Himself. In Christ He has done so most expressively. He has done so, that there might be no mistake as to His character on the part of man.

Christ's person is a revelation of God. Christ's work is a revelation of God. Christ's words are a revelation of God. He is in the Father, and the Father in Him. His words and works are the words and works of the Father. In the manger He showed us God. In the synagogue of Nazareth He showed us God. At Jacob's well He showed us God. At the tomb of Lazarus He showed us God. On Olivet, as He wept over Jerusalem, He showed us God. On the cross He showed us God. In the tomb He showed us God. In His resurrection He showed us God. If we say with Philip, "Shew us the Father, and it sufficeth us," He answers, "Have I been so long time with you, and yet hast thou not known me? He that hath seen me hath seen the Father" (Jn 14:8–9). This God whom Christ reveals, as the God of righteous grace and gracious righteousness, is the God with whom we have to do.

To know His character, as thus interpreted to us by Jesus and His cross, is to have peace. It is into this knowledge of the Father that the Holy Spirit leads the soul whom He is conducting, by His almighty power, from darkness to light. For, everything that we know of God we owe to this divine Teacher, this Interpreter. But never let the sinner imagine that he is more willing to learn than the Spirit is to teach. Never let him say to himself, "I would know God, but I cannot of myself, and the Spirit will not teach me."

It is not enough for us to say to a dispirited person, "It is your unbelief that is keeping you wretched; only believe, and all is well." This is true, but it is only general truth, which in many cases is of no use, because it does not show him how it applies to him. On this point he is often at fault, thinking that faith is some great work to be done, which he is to labour at with all his might, praying all the while to God to help him in doing this great work; and that unbelief is some evil principle requiring to be uprooted, before the gospel will be of any use to him.

But what is the real meaning of this faith and this unbelief?

In all unbelief there are these two things—a good opinion of one's self, and a bad opinion of God. So long as these two things exist, it is impossible for an inquirer to find rest. His good opinion of himself makes him think it quite possible to win God's favour by his own religious performances; and his bad opinion of God makes him unwilling and afraid to put his case wholly into His hands. The object of the Holy Spirit's work, in convincing of sin, is to alter the sinner's opinion of himself, and so to reduce his estimate of his own character that he shall think of himself as God does, and so cease to suppose it possible that he can be justified by any excellency of his own. Having altered the sinner's good opinion of himself, the Spirit then alters his evil opinion of God, so as to make him see that the God with whom he has to do is really the God of all grace.

But the inquirer denies that he has a good opinion of himself, and owns himself a sinner. Now, a man may say this; but really to know it is something more than saying. Besides, he may be willing to take the name of sinner to himself, in common with his fellowmen, and yet not at all own himself such a sinner as God says he is: such a sinner as needs a whole Saviour to himself; such a sinner as needs the cross, and blood, and righteousness of the Son of God. He may not have quite such a bad opinion of himself as to make him aware that he can expect nothing from God on the score of personal goodness, or amendment of life, or devout observance of duty, or superiority to others. It takes a great deal to destroy a man's good opinion of himself; and even after he has lost his good opinion of his works, he retains his good opinion of his heart; and even after he has lost that, he holds fast his good opinion of his religious duties, by means of which he hopes to make up for evil works and a bad heart. He hopes to be able so to act, and feel, and pray, as to lead God to entertain a good opinion of him, and receive him into favour.

All such efforts spring from thinking well of himself in some measure; and also from his thinking evil of God, as if He would not receive him as he is. If he knew himself as God does, he would no more resort to such efforts than he would think of walking up an Alpine precipice. How difficult it is to make a man think of himself as God does! What but the almightiness of the divine Spirit can accomplish this?

But the inquirer says that he has not a bad opinion of God. Has he, however, such an opinion of Him as the Bible gives, or the cross reveals? Has he such an opinion of Him as makes him feel quite safe in putting his soul into His gracious hands, and trusting Him with its eternal keeping? If not, where is his good opinion of God? Surely the knowledge of God, which the cross supplies, ought to set all doubt aside, and make distrust appear in the most odious of aspects, as a wretched misrepresentation of God's character and a slander upon His gracious name.

Unbelief is thus the belief of a lie and the rejection of the truth. It obliterates from the cross the gracious name of God, and inscribes another name, that of an unknown god, in which there is no peace for the sinner, no rest for the weary.

Accept, then, the character of God as given in the gospel; read aright His blessed name as it is written upon the cross; take the simple interpretation given of His mind toward the ungodly, as you have it, at length, in the glad tidings of peace. Is not that enough? If that which God has made known of Himself be not enough to allay your fears, nothing else will. The Holy Spirit will not give you peace, irrespective of your views of God's character. That would be countenancing the worship of a false god, instead of the true God revealed in the Bible. It is in connection with the truth concerning the true God, "the God of all grace," that the Spirit gives peace. It is the love of the true God that He sheds abroad in the heart.

The object of the Spirit's work is to make us acquainted with the true Jehovah, that in Him we may rest; not to produce in us certain feelings, the consciousness of which will make us think better of ourselves, and give us confidence toward God. That which He shows us of ourselves is only evil; that which He shows us of God is only good. He does not enable us to feel or to believe in order that we may be comforted by our feeling or our faith. Even when working in us most powerfully, He turns our eye away from His own work in us to fix it on God, and His love in Christ Jesus our Lord. The substance of the gospel is the name of the great Jehovah, unfolded in and by Jesus Christ, the character of Him in whom we "live and move and have our being," as the "just God" and the "Saviour" (Is 45:21), the Justifier of the ungodly.

Turn your eye to the cross and see these two things—the crucifiers and the Crucified. See the crucifiers, the haters of God and of His Son. They are yourself. Read in them your own character, and cease to think of making that a ground of peace. See the Crucified. It is God Himself, incarnate love. It is He who made you, God manifest in flesh, suffering, dying for the ungodly. Can you suspect His grace? Can you cherish evil thoughts of Him? Can you ask anything further to awaken in you the fullest and most unreserved confidence? Will you misinterpret that agony and death by saying either that they do not mean grace, or that the grace which they mean is not for you? Call to mind that which is written—"Hereby perceive we the love of God, because he laid down his life for us" (1 Jn 3:16). "Herein is love, not that we loved God, but that he loved us, and sent his Son to be the propitiation for our sins" (1 Jn 4:10).

4

Righteous Grace

We have spoken of God's character as "the God of all grace" (1 Pt 5:10). We have seen that it is in "tasting that the Lord is gracious" that the sinner has peace (1 Pt 2:3).

But let us keep in mind that this grace is the grace of a righteous God; it is the grace of one who is Judge as well as Father. Unless we see this we shall mistake the gospel, and fail in appreciating both the pardon we are seeking, and the great sacrifice through which it comes to us. No vague forgiveness, arising out of mere paternal love or good-natured indifference to sin, will do. We need to know what kind of pardon it is; and whether it proceeds from the full recognition of our absolute guiltiness, by Him who is to "judge the world in righteousness." The right kind of pardon comes not from love alone, but from law; not from good nature, but from righteousness; not from indifference to sin, but from holiness.

The inquirer who is only half in earnest overlooks this. His feelings are moved, but his conscience is not roused. Hence he is content with very vague ideas of God's mere compassion for the sinner's unhappiness. To him human guilt seems but human misfortune, and God's acquittal of the sinner little more than the overlooking of his sin. He does not trouble himself with asking how the forgiveness comes, or what is the real nature of the love which he professes to have received. He is easily soothed to sleep, because he has never been fully awake. He is, at the best, a stony-ground hearer, soon losing the poor measure of joy that he may have gotten; becoming a formalist, or perhaps a trifler with sin; or, it may be, a religious sentimentalist.

But he whose conscience has been pierced is not so easily satisfied. He sees that the God whose favour he is seeking is holy as well as loving, and that He has to do with righteousness as well as grace. Hence the first inquiry that he makes is as to the righteousness of the pardon which the grace of God holds out. He must be satisfied on this point, and see that the grace is righteous grace, before he can enjoy it at all. The more alive that he is to his own unrighteousness, the more does he feel the need of ascertaining the righteousness of the grace which we make known to him.

It does not satisfy him to say that, since it comes from a righteous God, it must be righteous grace. His conscience wants to see the righteousness of the way by which it comes. Without this it cannot be pacified or "purged"; and the man is not made "perfect as pertaining to the conscience" (Heb 9:9–14), but must always have an uneasy feeling that all is not right; that his sins may one day rise up against him.

That which soothes the heart will not always pacify the conscience. The sight of the grace will do the former; but only the sight of the righteousness of the grace will do the latter. Till the latter is done, there cannot be real peace.

Here the work of Christ comes in; and the cross of the Sin-bearer answers the question which conscience had raised—"Is it righteous grace?" It is this great work of propitiation that exhibits God as "the just God, and the Saviour" (Is 45:21), not only righteous in spite of His justifying the ungodly, but righteous in doing so. It shows salvation as an act of righteousness, indeed, one of the highest acts of righteousness that a righteous God can do. It shows pardon not only as the deed of a righteous God, but as *the* thing which declares how righteous He is, and how He hates and condemns the very sin that He is pardoning.

Hear the Word of the Lord concerning this "finished" work. "Christ died for our sins" (1 Cor 15:3). "He was wounded for our transgressions, he was bruised for our iniquities" (Is 53:5). "Christ was once offered to bear the sins of many" (Heb 9:28). "He gave himself for us" (Ti 2:14). He "was delivered for our offences" (Rom 4:25). He "gave himself for our sins" (Gal 1:4). "Christ died for the ungodly" (Rom 5:6). "He appeared to put away sin by the sacrifice of himself" (Heb 9:26). "Christ hath suffered for us in the flesh" (1 Pt 4:1). "Christ also hath once suffered for sins, the just for the unjust" (1 Pt 3:18). "His own self bare our sins in his own body on the tree" (1 Pt 2:24).

These expressions speak of something more than love. Love is in each of them—the deep, true, real love of God; but also justice and holiness—inflexible and inexorable adherence to law. They have no meaning apart from law; law as the foundation, pillar, and keystone of the universe.

But their connection with law is also their connection with love. For, as it was law, in its unchangeable perfection, that created the necessity for the Surety's death, so it was this necessity that drew out the Surety's love, and gave also glorious proof of the love of Him who made Him to be sin for us (2 Cor 5:21). For if a man were to die for another, when there was no necessity for his doing so, we should hardly call his death a proof of love. At best, such would be foolish love, or, at least, a fond and idle way of showing it. But to die for one, when there is really need of dying, is the true test of genuine love. To die for a friend when nothing less will save him, this is the proof of love! When either he or we must die, and when he, to save us from dying, dies himself, this is love. There was need of a death, if we were to be saved from dying. Righteousness made the necessity. And, to meet this terrible necessity, the Son of God took flesh and died! He died because it was written, "The soul that sinneth, it shall die" (Ezek 18:4). Love led Him down to the cradle; love led Him up to the cross! He died as the sinner's Substitute. He died to make it a righteous thing in God to cancel the sinner's guilt, and annul the penalty of his everlasting death.

Had it not been for this dying, grace and guilt could not have looked each other in the face; God and the sinner could not have come near; righteousness would have forbidden reconciliation; and righteousness, we know, is as divine and real a thing as love. Without this expiation, it would not have been right for God to receive the sinner, nor safe for the sinner to come.

But now, mercy and truth have met together (Ps 85:10); now grace is righteousness, and righteousness is grace. This satisfies the sinner's conscience by showing him righteous love for the unrighteous and unlovable. It tells him, too, that the reconciliation brought about in this way shall never be disturbed, either in this life or that which is to come. It is righteous reconciliation, and will stand every test, as well as last throughout eternity. The peace of conscience, thus secured, will be trial-proof, sickness-proof, deathbed-proof, judgment-proof. Realising this, the chief of sinners can say, "Who is he that condemneth?"

What peace for the stricken conscience is there in the truth that Christ died for the *ungodly* and that it is of the *ungodly* that the righteous God is the Justifier! The righteous grace, thus coming to us through the sin-bearing work of the "Word made flesh," tells the soul, at once and for ever, that there can be no condemnation for any sinner upon earth who will only consent to be indebted to this free love of God, which, like a fountain of living water, is bursting out freely from the foot of the cross.

Just, yet the Justifier of the ungodly! What glad tidings are here! Here is grace—God's free love to the sinner—divine bounty and goodwill, altogether irrespective of human worth or merit. For this is the scriptural meaning of that often misunderstood word "grace."

This righteous free love has its origin in the bosom of the Father, where the only-begotten Son has His dwelling (Jn 1:18). It is not produced by anything outside of God Himself. It was man's evil, not his good, that called it forth. It is not the like drawing to the like, but to the unlike; it is light attracted by darkness, and life by death. It does not wait for our seeking, it comes unasked as well as undeserved. It is not our faith that creates it or calls it up; our faith realises it as already existing, in its divine and manifold fullness. Whether we believe it or not, this righteous grace exists, and exists for us. Unbelief refuses it; but faith takes it, rejoices in it, and lives upon it.

Yes, faith takes this righteous grace of God, and with it a righteous pardon, a righteous salvation, and a righteous heirship of the everlasting glory.

5

The Blood of Sprinkling

But an inquirer asks, What is the special meaning of the blood, of which we read so much? How does it speak of peace? How does it "purge the conscience from dead works" (Heb 9:14)? What can blood have to do with the peace, the grace, and the righteousness of which we have been speaking?

God has given the reason for the stress which He lays upon the blood; and, in understanding this, we get to the very bottom of the grounds of a sinner's peace.

The sacrifices of old, from the days of Abel onwards, furnish us with the key to the meaning of the blood, and explain the necessity for its being "shed for the remission of sins." "Not without blood" (Heb 9:7) was the great truth taught by God from the beginning; the inscription which may be said to have been written on the gates of tabernacle and temple. For more than two thousand years, during the ages of the patriarchs, there was but one great sacrifice—the burnt offering. This, under the Mosaic service, was split into parts—the peace offering, trespass offering, and sin-offering. In all of these, however, the essence of the original burnt offering was preserved—by the blood and the fire which were common to them all. The blood, as the emblem of substitution, and the fire, as the symbol of God's wrath upon the substitute, were seen in all the parts of Israel's service; but especially in the daily burnt offering—the morning and evening lamb—which was the true continuation and representative of the old patriarchal burnt offering. It was to this that John referred when he said, "Behold the Lamb of God, which taketh away the sin of the world" (Jn 1:29). Israel's daily lamb was the kernel and core of all the Old Testament sacrifices, and it was its blood that carried the worshippers back to the primitive sacrifices, and forward to the blood of sprinkling that was to speak better things than that of Abel (Heb 12:24).

In all these sacrifices the shedding of the blood was the infliction of death. The "blood was the life" (Lv 17:11, 14; Dt 12:23), and the pouring out of the blood was "the pouring out of the soul" (Is 53:12). This blood shedding or life taking was the payment of the penalty for sin; for it was threatened from the beginning, "In the day that thou eatest thereof thou shalt surely die" (Gn 2:17); and it is written, "The soul that sinneth, it shall die" (Ezek 18:4); and again, "The wages of sin is death" (Rom 6:23).

But the blood shedding of Israel's sacrifices could not take sin away. It showed the way in which this was to be done, but it was in fact more a "remembrance of sins" (Heb 10:3) than an expiation (Heb 10:11). It said life must be given for life, before sin can be pardoned; but then the continual repetition of the sacrifices showed that there was needed "richer blood" than the temple altar was ever sprinkled with and a more precious life than man could give.

The great blood shedding has been accomplished; the better life has been presented, and the one death of the Son of God has done what all the deaths of old could never do. His one life was enough; His one dying paid the penalty; and God does not ask two lives, or two deaths, or two payments. "Christ was once offered to bear the sins of many" (Heb 9:28). "In that he died, he died unto sin once" (Rom 6:10). He "offered one sacrifice for sins for ever" (Heb 10:12).

The "sprinkling of the blood" (Ex 24:8) was the making use of the death by putting it upon certain persons or things, so that these persons or things were counted to be dead, and therefore, to have paid the law's penalty. So long as they had not paid that penalty, they were counted unclean and unfit for God to look upon; but as soon as they had paid it, they were counted clean and fit for the service of God. Usually when we read of cleansing, we think merely of our common process of removing dirt by water and soap. But this is not the figure meant in the application of the sacrifice. The blood cleanses by making us partakers of the death of the Substitute. For what is it that makes us filthy before God? It is our guilt, our breach of law, and our being under sentence of death in consequence of our disobedience. We have not only done what God dislikes, but what His righteous law declares to be worthy of death. It is this sentence of death that separates us so completely from God, making it wrong for Him to bless us, and perilous for us to go to Him.

When thus covered all over with that guilt whose penalty is death, the blood is brought in by the great High Priest. That blood represents death; it is God's expression for death. It is then sprinkled on us, and thus death, which is the law's penalty, passes on us. We die. We undergo the sentence, and thus the guilt passes away. We are cleansed! The sin which was like scarlet becomes as snow, and that which was like crimson becomes as wool. It is thus that we make use of the blood of Christ in believing, for faith is just the sinner employing the blood. Believing what God has testified concerning this blood, we become one with Jesus in His death; and thus we are counted in law, and treated by God, as men who have paid the whole penalty, and so been "washed from their sins in his blood."

Such are the glad tidings of life, through Him who died. They are tidings which tell us, not what we are to do, in order to be saved, but what He has done. This only can lay to rest the sinner's fears, can "purge his conscience," can make him feel as a thoroughly pardoned man. The right knowledge of God's meaning in this sprinkling of the blood is the only effective way of removing the anxieties of the troubled soul, and introducing it into perfect peace.

The gospel is not the mere revelation of the heart of God in Christ Jesus. In it the righteousness of God is specially manifested (Rom 1:17); and it is this revelation of the righteousness that makes it so truly "the power of God unto salvation" (Rom 1:16). The blood shedding is God's declaration of the righteousness of the love which He is pouring down upon the sons of men; it is the reconciliation of law and love; the condemnation of the sin and the acquittal of the sinner. As "without shedding of blood there is no remission" (Heb 9:22), so the gospel announces that the blood has been shed by which remission flows to us; and now we know that "the blood of Christ cleanses us from all sin" (1 Jn 1:7). The conscience is satisfied. It feels that God's grace is righteous grace, that His love is holy love. There it rests.

It is not by incarnation but by blood shedding that we are saved. The Christ of God is no mere expounder of wisdom, no mere deliverer or gracious benefactor; and they who think that they have told the whole gospel, when they have spoken of Jesus revealing the love of God, greatly err.

If Christ is not the Substitute, He is nothing to the sinner. If He did not die as the Sin-bearer, He has died in vain. Let us not be deceived on this point, nor misled by those who, when they announce Christ as the Deliverer, think they have preached the gospel. If I throw a rope to a drowning man, I am a deliverer. But is Christ no more than that? If I cast myself into the sea, and risk myself to save another, I am a deliverer. But is Christ no more? Did He but risk His life? The very essence of Christ's deliverance is the substitution of Himself for us, His life for ours. He did not come to risk His life; He came to die! He did not redeem us by a little loss, a little sacrifice, a little labour, a little suffering: "He redeemed us to God by his blood," "the precious blood of Christ" (1 Pt 1:19). He gave all He had, even His life, for us. This is the kind of deliverance that awakens the happy song, "To him that loved us, and washed us from our sins in his own blood" (Rv 1:5; 5:9).

The tendency of the world's religion just now is to reject the blood, and to glory in a gospel which needs no sacrifice, no "Lamb slain." Thus, they go the way of Cain, who refused the blood, and came to God without it. He would not own himself a sinner, condemned to die, and needing the death of another to save him. This was man's open rejection of God's way of life. Foremost in this rejection we see the first murderer; and he who would not defile his altar with the blood of a lamb pollutes the earth with his brother's blood.

The heathen altars have been red with blood; and to this day they are the same. But these worshippers do not know what they mean in bringing that blood. It is associated only with vengeance in their minds; and they shed it to appease the vengeance of their gods. But this is no recognition either of the love or the righteousness of God. "Fury is not in him," whereas their altars speak only of fury. The blood which they bring is a denial both of righteousness and grace.

But look at Israel's altars. There is blood; and they who bring it know the God to whom they come. They bring it in acknowledgment of their own guilt, but also of His pardoning love. They say, "I deserve death; but let this death stand for mine; and let the love which otherwise could not reach me, by reason of guilt, now pour itself out on me."

Beware of Cain's error on the one hand, in coming to God

without blood; and beware of the heathen error on the other, in mistaking the meaning of the blood. Understand God's mind and meaning in "the precious blood" of His Son. Believe His testimony concerning it; so shall your conscience be pacified, and your soul find rest.

It is into Christ's death that we are baptized (Rom 6:3), and hence the cross, which was the instrument of that death, is that in which we glory. The cross is to us the payment of the sinner's penalty, the extinction of the debt, and the tearing up of the handwriting which was against us. And as the cross is the payment, so the resurrection is God's receipt in full, for the whole sum, signed with His own hand. Our faith is not the completion of the payment, but the simple recognition on our part of the payment made by the Son of God. By this recognition we become so one with Him who died and rose, that we are thereafter reckoned to be the parties who have paid the penalty, and treated as if it were we ourselves who had died. Thus are we "justified from sin," and then made partakers of the righteousness of Him, who was not only delivered for our offences, but who was raised again for our justification.

6

The Person and Work of the Substitute

Life comes to us through death; and thus grace abounds towards us in righteousness. This we have seen in a general way. But we have something more to learn concerning Him who lived and died as the sinner's Substitute. The more that we know of His person and His work, the more shall we be satisfied, in heart and conscience, with the provision which God has made for our great need.

Our Sin-bearer is the eternal Son of God. Of Him it is written, "In the beginning was the Word, and the Word was with God, and the Word was God" (Jn 1:1). He is "the brightness of his glory, and the express image of his person" (Heb 1:3). He is "in the Father, and the Father in him"; "the Father dwelleth in him"; "he that hath seen him hath seen the Father" (Jn 14:9–11); and "he that heareth him, heareth him that sent him." He is "the Word made flesh" (Jn 1:14); "God manifest in the flesh" (1 Tm

3:16); "Jesus the Christ, who has come in the flesh" (1 Jn 4:2–3). His name is "Immanuel," God with us (Is 7:14; Mt 1:23); Jesus, the "Saviour" (Mt 1:21); "Christ," the anointed One, filled with the Spirit without measure (Jn 3:34); "the only-begotten of the Father, full of grace and truth" (Jn 1:14).

He came preaching "the gospel of the kingdom," that is, the good news about the kingdom (Mk 1:14); teaching the multitudes that gathered round Him (Mk 4:1); healing the sick, opening the eyes of the blind, and raising the dead (Mt 4:23, 24); "receiving sinners, and eating with them" (Lk 15:2). He "came to seek and save that which was lost" (Lk 19:10); He went about speaking words of grace such as never man spoke, saying, "I am the Way, and the Truth, and the Life: no man cometh unto the Father, but by me" (Jn 14:6).

He went out and in, as the Saviour; and in His whole life we see Him, as the shepherd seeking his lost sheep, as the woman searching for her lost piece of silver, and as the father looking out for his lost son. He is "mighty to save" (Is 63:1); He is "able to save to the uttermost" (Heb 7:25); He came to be "the Saviour of the world" (1 Jn 4:14).

In all these things, thus written concerning Jesus, there is good news for the sinner, such as should draw him, in simple confidence, to God; making him feel that his case has really been taken up in earnest by God; and that God's thoughts toward him are thoughts, not of anger, but of peace and grace. Heaven has come down to earth! There is goodwill toward man. He is not to be handed over to his great enemy. God has taken his side, and stepped in between him and Satan. This world is not to be destroyed, nor all its dwellers made eternal exiles from God! The darkness is passing away, and the true light is shining!

Yet it is not the person of Christ, nor His birth, nor His life, that can suffice. That the Son of God took a true but sinless humanity, of the very substance of the virgin; becoming bone of our bone, and flesh of our flesh; being in very deed the woman's seed; that He dwelt among us for a lifetime, is but the beginning of the good news; the Alpha but not the Omega. This was shown to Israel, and to us also, in the temple veil. That veil was the type of His flesh (Heb 10:20); and, so long as that curtain remained whole, there was no entrance into the place of the near presence of God. The worshipper was not indeed frowned upon; but he had to stand at a distance. The veil said to the sinner, Godhead is within; but it also said, You cannot enter till something more has been done. The Holy Ghost, by it, signified that the way into the holiest was not yet open. The rending of the veil, that is the crucifixion of "the Word made flesh," opened the way completely.

Hence it is that the Holy Spirit sums up the good news in one or two special points. They are these. Christ was crucified. Christ died. Christ was buried. Christ arose again from the dead. Christ went up on high. Christ sits at God's right hand, our "Advocate with the Father" (1 Jn 2:1), "ever living to make intercession for us" (Rom 8:34; Heb 7:25).

These are the great facts which contain the good news. They are few, and they are plain, so that a child may remember and understand them. They are the caskets which contain the heavenly gems. They are the cups which hold the living water for the thirsty soul, the golden basket in which God has placed the bread of life, the true bread which came down from heaven, of which if a man eat he shall never die. They are the volumes in whose brief but precious pages are written the records of God's mighty mercy; records so simple that even a "fool" may read and comprehend them; so true and sure that all the wisdom of the world, and all the wiles of hell, cannot shake their certainty.

The knowledge of these is salvation. On them we rest our confidence; for they are the revelation of the name of God; and it is written, "They that know thy name will put their trust in thee" (Ps 9:10).

Let us listen to apostolic preaching, and see how these facts form the heads of the first sermons, sermons such as Peter's at Jerusalem, or Paul's at Corinth and Antioch. Peter's sermon at Jerusalem (Acts 2:29–36) was that Jesus of Nazareth, who was crucified, had been raised from the dead, and exalted to the throne of God, being made both Lord and Christ. This the apostle declared to be "good news." Paul's sermon at Antioch was in substance the same: a statement of the facts regarding the death and resurrection of Jesus; and the application of that sermon was in these words, "Be it known unto you, men and brethren, that through this man is preached unto you the forgiveness of sins: and by him all that believe are justified" (Acts 13:38, 39). He gives us elsewhere the following sketch of his preaching: "Moreover, brethren, I declare unto you the gospel which I preached unto you, . . . how that Christ died for our sins according to the Scriptures; and that he was buried, and that he rose again the third day according to the Scriptures" (1 Cor 15:1–4). Then he adds: "So we preach, and so ye believed" (v. 11).

Such was apostolic preaching. Such was Paul's gospel. It narrated a few facts respecting Christ, adding the evidence of their truth and certainty, that all who heard might believe and be saved. In these facts the free love of God to sinners is announced; and the great salvation is revealed. It is this gospel which is "the power of God unto salvation to every one that believeth. . . . For therein is the righteousness of God revealed from faith to faith" (Rom 1:16, 17).

Its burden was not, "Do this, or do that; labour and pray, and use the means"—that is law, not gospel; but Christ has done all! He did it all when He was "delivered for our offences, and raised again for our justification" (Rom 4:25). He did it all when He "made peace by the blood of his cross" (Col 1:20). "It is finished" (Jn 19:30). His doing is so complete that it has left nothing for us to do. We have but to enter into the joy of knowing that all is done! "This is the record, that God hath given to us eternal life, and this life is in his Son" (1 Jn 5:11).

But let us gather together some of the true "sayings of God" concerning Christ and His work. In these we shall find the divine interpretation of the facts above referred to. We shall see the meaning which the Holy Spirit attaches to these, and so our faith shall not "stand in the wisdom of men, but in the power of God" (1 Cor 2:5). It was in this way that the Lord Himself, before He left the earth, removed the unbelief of the doubters around Him. He reminded them of the written word, "Thus it is written, and thus it behooved [the] Christ to suffer, and to rise from the dead the third day: and that repentance and remission of sins should be preached in his name among all nations, beginning at Jerusalem" (Luke 24:46–47).

Hear, then, the Word of the Lord! For heaven and earth shall pass away, but these words shall not pass away:

"God hath not appointed us to wrath, but to obtain salvation by our Lord Jesus Christ, who died for us, that, whether we wake or sleep, we should live together with him" (1 Th 5:9–10). "By the which will we are sanctified through the offering of the body of Jesus Christ once for all" (Heb 10:10). "In due time Christ died for the ungodly" (Rom 5:6). "It is Christ that died, yea rather, that is risen again, who is even at the right hand of God, who also maketh intercession for us" (Rom 8:34). "Who gave himself for our sins" (Gal 1:4). "Christ hath redeemed us from the curse of the law, being made a curse for us" (Gal 3:13). "In whom we have redemption through his blood, the forgiveness of sins, according to the riches of his grace" (Eph 1:7).

"He humbled himself, and became obedient unto death, even the death of the cross" (Phil 2:8). "Remember that Jesus Christ of the seed of David was raised from the dead according to my gospel" (2 Tm 2:8). "Who gave himself for us" (Ti 2:14). "Christ was once offered to bear the sins of many" (Heb 9:28). "Jesus also, that he might sanctify the people with his own blood, suffered without the gate" (Heb 13:12). "Christ also suffered for us" (1 Pt 2:21). "Who his own self bare our sins in his own body on the tree" (1 Pt 2:24). "Christ also hath once suffered for sins, the just for the unjust" (1 Pt 3:18). "Christ hath suffered for us in the flesh" (1 Pt 4:1). "He is the propitiation for our sins" (1 Jn 2:2). "Unto him that loved us, and washed us from our sins in his own blood" (Rv 1:5). "I am he that liveth, and was dead; and behold, I am alive for evermore" (Rv 1:18). "Thou wast slain, and hast redeemed us to God by thy blood" (Rv 5:9).

These are all divine truths, written in divine words. These sayings are faithful and true; they come from Him that cannot lie; and they are as true in these last days as they were when first written; for "the word of our God shall stand for ever" (Is 40:8; 1 Pt 1:25). In them we find the authentic exposition of the facts which the apostles preached; and, in that, we learn the glad tidings concerning the way in which salvation from a righteous God has come to unrighteous man. Jesus died—that is the paying of the debt, the endurance of the penalty, the death for death. He was buried—that is the proof that His death was a true death, needing a tomb as we do. He rose again—this is God's declaration that He, the righteous Judge, is satisfied with the payment, no less than with Him who made it.

Could there be better, gladder news to the sinner than this? What more can he ask to satisfy him than that which has so fully satisfied the holy Lord God of earth and heaven? If this will not avail, then he can expect no more. If this is not enough, then Christ has died in vain.

God has thus "brought near his righteousness" (Is 46:13). We do not need to go up to heaven for it; that would imply that Christ had never come down. Nor do we need to go down to the depths of the earth for it; that would say that Christ had never been buried and never risen. It is near. It is as near as is the word concerning it, which enters into our ears (Rom 10:8). We do not need to exert ourselves to bring it near, nor to do anything to attract it towards us. It is already so near, so very near, that we cannot bring it closer. If we try to get up warm feelings and good dispositions, in order to remove some fancied remainder of distance, we shall fail; not simply because these actings of ours cannot do what we are trying to do, but because there is no need of any such effort. The thing is done already. God has brought His righteousness near to the sinner. The office of faith is not to work, but to cease working; not to do anything, but to own that all is done; not to bring near the righteousness, but to rejoice in it as already near. This is "the word of the truth of the gospel" (Col 1:5).

7

The Word of the Truth of the Gospel

How shall I come before God, and stand in His presence, with happy confidence on my part, and gracious acceptance on His?

This is the sinner's question; and he asks it because he knows that there is guilt between him and God. No doubt this was Adam's question when he stitched his fig leaves together for a covering. But he was soon made to feel that the fig leaves would not do. He must be wholly covered, not in part only; and that by something which even God's eye cannot see through. As God comes near, the uselessness of his fig leaves is felt, and he rushes into the thick foliage to hide from the divine eye. The Lord approaches the trembling man, and makes him feel that this hiding place will not do. Then He begins to tell him what will do. He announces a better covering and a better hiding-place. He reveals Himself as the God of grace, the God who hates sin, yet who takes the sinner's side against the sinner's enemy, the old serpent. And all this through the seed of the woman, "the man" who is the true "hiding place" (Is 32:2). Adam can now leave his thicket safely, and feel that in this revealed grace he can stand before God without fear or shame. He has heard the good news, and brief as it is, it has restored his confidence and removed his alarm.

Let us hear the good news, and let us hear it as Adam did—from the lips of God Himself. For that which is revealed for our belief is set before us on God's authority, not on man's. We are not only to believe the truth, but we are to believe it because God has spoken it. Faith must have a divine foundation.

We gather together a few of these divine announcements, asking the reader to study them as divine. Nor let him say that he knows them already; but let him accept our invitation to traverse, along with us, the field of gospel statement. It is of God Himself that we must learn; and it is only by listening to the very words of God that we shall arrive at the true knowledge of what the gospel is. His own words are the truest, the simplest, and the best. They are not only the most likely to meet our case; but they are the words which He has promised to honour and bless.

Let us hear, then, the words of God as to His own grace, or free love, or mercy:

"The LORD passed by before him, and proclaimed, The LORD, The LORD God, merciful and gracious, long-suffering, and abundant in goodness and truth, keeping mercy for thousands, forgiving iniquity and transgression and sin" (Ex 34:6–7). "The LORD is long-suffering, and of great mercy (Nm 14:18). "His mercies are great" (2 Sm 24:14). "The LORD your God is gracious and merciful (2 Chr 30:9). "Thou art a God ready to pardon, gracious and merciful" (Neh 9:17). "His mercy endureth for ever (1 Chr 16:34). "Thou, Lord, art good, and ready to forgive; and plenteous in mercy unto all them that call upon thee" (Ps 86:5); "Thou, O Lord, art a God full of compassion, and gracious, long-suffering, and plenteous in mercy and truth" (Ps 86:15); "thy mercy is great unto the heavens" (Ps 57:10); "thy mercy is great above the heavens" (Ps 108:4); "his tender mercies are over all his works" (Ps 145:9).

"Who is a God like unto thee, that pardoneth iniquity, and passeth by the transgression of the remnant of his heritage? he retaineth not his anger for ever, because he delighteth in mercy" (Mi 7:18); "I will love them freely" (Hos 14:4); "God so loved the world, that he gave his only begotten Son" (Jn 3:16); "God commendeth his love toward us" (Rom 5:8); "God, who is rich in mercy, for his great love wherewith he hath loved us, even when we were dead in sins" (Eph 2:4); "the kindness and love of God our Saviour toward man" (Ti 3:4); "according to his mercy he saved us" (Ti 3:5); "In this was manifested the love of God toward us, because that God sent his only begotten Son into the world, that we might live through him; herein is love, not that we loved God, but that he loved us, and sent his Son to be the propitiation for our sins" (1 Jn 4:9–10); "the only begotten of the Father, full of grace and truth" (Jn 1:14); "grace and truth came by Jesus Christ" (Jn 1:17); "the word of his grace" (Acts 14:3); "the gospel of the grace of God" (Acts 20:24).

Such are a few of the words of Him who cannot lie concerning His own grace, or free love. These sayings are faithful and true; and though perhaps we may but little have owned them as such, or heeded the truth which they embody, yet they are fitted to speak peace to the soul even of the most troubled. Each of these words of grace is like a star sparkling in the blue sky above us; or like a well of water pouring out its freshness amid desert rocks and sands.

Let no one say, "We know all these passages. Of what use is it to read and re-read words so familiar?" Of great use! Chiefly because it is in such declarations regarding the riches of God's free love that the gospel is wrapped up; and it is out of these that the Holy Spirit ministers light and peace to us. Such are the words which He delights to honour as His messengers of joy to the soul. Hear then, in these, the voice of the Spirit's love, as well as the love of the Father and the Son! If you find no peace coming out of them to you as you read them the first time, read them again. If you find nothing the second time, read them once more. If you find nothing the hundredth or the thousandth time, study them yet again. "The word of God is quick [living], and powerful" (Heb 4:12); His sayings are the "lively oracles" (Acts 7:38); "his word liveth and abideth for ever" (1 Pt 1:23); it is "like as a fire . . . and like a hammer that breaketh the rock in pieces" (Jer 23:29). The gospel is "the power of God" (Rom 1:16); and it is "by manifestation of the truth" that we commend ourselves to every man's conscience in the sight of God (2 Cor 4:2).

There are no words like those of God, in heaven or in earth. Hence it is that you are to study "that which is written"; for He Himself wrote it; and He wrote it for you. Do not think it needless to read these passages again and again. They will blaze up at last, and light up that dark soul of yours with the very joy of heaven.

You have sometimes looked up to the sky at twilight, searching for a star which you expected to find in its usual place. You did not see it at first, but you knew it was there, and that its light was undiminished. So instead of closing your eye or turning away to some other object, you continued to gaze more and more intently on the spot where you knew it was. Slowly and faintly the star seemed to come out in the sky as you gazed; and your persevering search ended in the discovery of the long-sought gem.

So it is with those passages which speak to you of the free love of God. You say, "I have looked into them, but they contain nothing for me." Do not turn away from them as if you knew them so well already that you could find nothing new in them. You have not seen them yet. There are wonders beyond all price hidden in each one. Take them up again. Search and study them. The Holy Spirit is most willing to reveal to you the glory which they contain. It is His office, it is His delight to be the sinner's Teacher. He will not be behind you in willingness. It is of the utmost moment that you should remember this lest you should grieve and repel Him by your distrust.

Never lose sight of this great truth that the evil thing in you, which is the root of bitterness to the soul, is distrust of God; distrust of the Father, who so loved the world as to give His Son; distrust of the Son, who came to seek and save that which was lost; distrust of the Holy Ghost, whose tender mercies are over you, and whose work of love is to reveal the Christ of God to your souls.

Besides, keep this in mind that, in teaching you, He is honouring His own Word and glorifying Christ. You need not then suspect Him of indifference toward you, or doubt His willingness to "enlighten the eyes of your understanding." While you are firmly persuaded that it is only His teaching that can be of any real use to you, do not grieve Him by separating His love in writing the Bible for you from His willingness to make you understand it. He who gave you the Word will interpret it for you. He does not stand aloof from you or from His own Word, as if He needed to be persuaded, or bribed by your deeds and prayers, to unfold the heavenly truth to you. Trust Him for teaching. Avail yourself at once of His love and power. Do not say, I am not entitled to trust Him till I am converted. You are to trust Him as a sinner, not as a converted man. You are to trust him as you are, not as you hope to be made before long. Your conversion is not your warrant for trusting Him.

The great sin of an unconverted man is his not trusting the God that made him, Father, Son, and Spirit. And how can anyone be so foolish, not to say wicked, as to ask for a warrant for forsaking sin? What would you say to a thief who said, "I have no warrant to forsake stealing; I must wait till I am made an honest man; then I shall give it up"? And what shall I say to a distruster of God, who tells me that he has no warrant for giving up his distrust, for he is not entitled to trust God till he is converted? One of the greatest things in conversion is turning from distrust to trust. If you are not entitled to turn at once from distrust to trust, then your distrust is not sin. If, however, your distrust of the Holy Spirit be one of your worst sins, how absurd it is to say, I am not entitled to trust Him till I am converted! For is not that just saying, I am not entitled to trust Him till I trust Him?

You say that you know God is gracious, yet, by your acting, you show that you do not believe Him to be so; or, at least, to be so gracious as to be willing to show you the meaning of His own Word. You believe Him to be so gracious as to give His only begotten Son; yet the way in which you treat Him, as to His Word, shows that you do not believe He is willing to give His Spirit to make known His truth. You think yourself much more willing to be taught than He is to teach; more willing to be blessed than He is to bless.

You say, "I must wait till God enlightens my mind." If God had told you that waiting is the way to light, you would be right. But He has nowhere told you to wait; and your idea of waiting is a mere excuse for not trusting Him immediately. If your way of proceeding be correct, God must have said both "Come" and "Wait"; "Come now, but do not come now," which is a contradiction.

When a kind rich man sends a message to a poor cripple to come at once to him and be provided for, he sends his carriage to convey him. He does not say, "Come; but then, as you are lame, and have besides no means of conveyance, you must use all the means in your power to induce me to send my carriage for you." The invitation and the carriage go together.

Much more is this true of God and His messages. His Word and His Spirit go together. Not that the Spirit is *in* the Word, or the power *in* the message, as some foolishly tell you. They are distinct things, but they go together. And your mistake lies in supposing that He who sent the one may not be willing to send the other. You think that it is He, not yourself, who creates the interval which you call "waiting"; although this waiting is, in reality, a deliberate refusal to comply with a command of God, and a determination to do something else, which He has not commanded, instead; a determination to make the doing of that something else an excuse for not doing the very thing commanded! Thus it is that you rid yourself of blame by pleading inability; in fact, you throw the blame on God for not being willing to do immediately that which He is most willing to do.

God demands immediate acceptance of His Son, and immediate belief of His gospel. You evade this duty on the plea that, as you cannot accept Christ of yourself, you must go and ask Him to enable you to do so. By this pretext, you try to relieve yourself from the overwhelming sense of the necessity for immediate obedience. You soothe your conscience with the idea that you are doing what you can, in the meantime, and that thus you are not so guilty of unbelief as before, seeing you desire to believe, and are doing your part in this great business!

It will not do. The command is, "Believe on the Lord Jesus Christ." Nothing less than this is pleasing to God. And though it is every man's duty to pray, just as it is every man's duty to love God, and to keep His statutes, yet you must not delude yourself with the idea that you are doing the right thing when you only pray to believe, instead of believing. The thief may desire to give up stealing, and pray to be enabled to give it up; yet he is still a thief until he actually gives it up.

The question is not as to whether prayer is a duty, but whether it is a right and acceptable thing to pray in unbelief. It is every man's duty to pray; and it is absurd, as it is unscriptural, to say that a man's being unconverted releases him from this duty. But the real point which we press home upon the sinner is this: Is it to believing or unbelieving prayer that God is calling you? Unbelieving prayer is prayer to an unknown God, and it cannot be your duty to pray to an unknown God.

You must get on your knees, believing either that God is willing, or that He is not willing, to bless you. In the latter case, you cannot expect any answer or blessing. In the former case, you are really, though unconsciously, believing already; as it is written, "He that cometh to God must believe that he is, and that he is a rewarder of them that diligently seek him" (Heb 11:6). In maintaining the duty of praying before believing, you cannot surely be asserting that it is your duty to go to God in unbelief? Are you to persist in unbelief till, in some miraculous way, faith drops into you, and God compels you to believe? Must you go to God with unacceptable prayer, in order to induce Him to give you the power of acceptable prayer? Is this what you mean by the duty of praying in order to believe? If so, it is a delusion and a sin.

Understanding prayer in the scriptural sense, I would tell every man to pray, just as I would tell every man to believe. For prayer includes and presupposes faith. It assumes that the man knows something of the God he is going to; and that is faith. "Whosoever shall call upon the name of the Lord shall be saved" (Rom 10:13). But then the apostle adds, "How shall they call on him in whom they have not believed?" (v. 14). Does not this last verse go to the very root of the matter before us? It is every man's duty to "call upon the name of the Lord" (Joel 2:32; Acts 2:21); indeed, it is the great sin of the ungodly that they do not do so (Ps 14:4; Jer 10:25). Yet says the apostle, "How shall they call on him in whom they have not believed?"

But I do not enter further on this point here. It may come up again. Meanwhile, I would just remind you concerning God's free love, in the free gift of His Son. Listen to what He Himself has told you regarding this, and know the God who is asking you to call upon His name; for if you but knew this God and His great gift of love, you would ask of Him, and He would give you living water (Jn 4:10). Remember that the gospel is not a list of duties to be performed, or feelings to be produced, or a frame of mind which we are to pray ourselves into, in order to make God think well of us, and in order to fit us for receiving pardon. The gospel is the good news of the great work done upon the cross. The knowledge of that finished work is immediate peace.

Read again and again the wonderful words which I have quoted at length from His own Book. The Bible is a living Book, not a dead one; a divine one, not a human one; a perfect one, not an imperfect one.

Search it, study it, dig into it. "My son," says God, our Father, "receive my words; hide my commandments with thee; incline thine ear unto wisdom; take fast hold of instruction; attend unto my wisdom, and bow thine ear to my understanding; keep my words, and lay up my commandments with thee." Do not say these messages are only for the children of God; for, as if to prevent this, God thus speaks to the "simple," the "scorners," the "fools," "Turn ye at my reproof," showing us that it is in listening to His words that the simple, the scorner, and the fool cease to be such, and become sons. Do not revert to the old difficulty about your need of the Holy Spirit; for, as if to meet this, God, in the above passage, adds, "Behold, I will pour out my Spirit unto you, I will make known my words unto you" (Prv 1:23). Not for one moment would God allow you to suspect His willingness to accompany His Word with His Spirit.

Honour the words of God;[1] and honour Him who wrote them by trusting Him for interpretation and light. Do not disparage them by calling them "a dead letter." They are not dead. If you will use the figure of "death" in this case, use it rightly. They are "the savour of death unto death in them that perish"; but this

---

1. "We must make a great difference between God's word and the word of man. Man's word is a little sound which flies into the air, and soon vanishes; but the word of God is greater than heaven and earth, yea, it is greater than death and hell, for it is the power of God, and remains everlastingly. Therefore we ought diligently to learn God's word, and we must know certainly and believe that God Himself speaks with us." Martin Luther, *Table Talk*, section 44.

only shows their vitality. As the blood of Christ either cleanses or condemns, so the words of the Spirit either kill or make alive.

Again I say to you, honour the words of God. Make much of them. "Them that honour me I will honour," is as true of Scripture as it is of the God of Scripture. Peace, light, comfort, life, salvation, holiness, are wrapped up in them. "Thy word hath quickened me" (Ps 119:50). "I will never forget thy precepts: for with them thou hast quickened me" (Ps 119:93).

It is through "belief of the truth that God hath from the beginning chosen us to salvation" (2 Th 2:13). It is "with the word of truth" that He begets us (Jas 1:18); and all this is in perfect harmony with the great truth of man's total helplessness, and his need of the almighty Spirit.

"So then faith cometh by hearing, and hearing by the word of God (Rom 10:17). "Hear, and your soul shall live" (Is 55:3).

8

Believe and Be Saved

It is the Holy Spirit alone that can draw us to the cross, and fasten us to the Saviour. He who thinks he can do without the Spirit has yet to learn his own sinfulness and helplessness. The gospel would be no good news to the dead in sin if it did not tell of the love and power of the divine Spirit as explicitly as it announces the love and power of the divine Substitute.

But, while keeping this in mind, we may try to learn from Scripture what is written concerning the bond which connects us individually with the cross of Christ, thereby making us partakers of the pardon and the life which that cross reveals.

Thus then it is written, "By grace are ye saved, through faith, and that not of yourselves; it is the gift of God" (Eph 2:8).

Faith, then, is the link, the one link, between the sinner and the Sin-bearer. It is not faith as a work or exercise of our minds, which must be properly performed in order to qualify or fit us for pardon. It is not faith as a religious duty, which must be gone through according to certain rules in order to induce Christ to give us the benefits of His work. It is faith simply as a receiver of the divine record concerning the Son of God. It is not faith considered as the source of holiness, as containing in itself the seed of all spiritual excellence and good works; it is faith alone, recognising simply the completeness of the great sacrifice for sin, and the trueness of the Father's testimony to that completeness; as Paul writes to the Thessalonians, "our testimony among you was believed" (2 Th 1:10). It is not faith as a piece of money or a thing of merit; but faith taking God at His word, and giving Him credit for speaking the honest truth, when He declares that "Christ died for the ungodly" (Rom 5:6), and that the life which that death contains for sinners is to be had "without money, and without price" (Is 55:1).

But let us learn about this faith from the lips of God Himself. I lay great stress on this in dealing with inquirers. For the more that we can fix the sinner's eye and conscience upon God's own words, the more likely shall we be to lead him aright, and to secure the quickening presence of that almighty Spirit who alone can give sight to the blind. One great difficulty which the inquirer finds is that of unlearning much of his past experience and teaching. Hence the importance of studying the divine words themselves, by which the sinner is made wise unto salvation. For they both unteach the false and imperfect, and teach the true and the perfect.

Let us see how frequently and strongly God has spoken respecting "faith" and "believing." "Without faith it is impossible to please God" (Heb 11:6). "Therein is the righteousness of God revealed from faith to faith: as it is written, The just shall live by faith" (Rom 1:17). "The righteousness of God which is by faith of Jesus Christ unto all and upon all them that believe" (Rom 3:22). "Whom God hath set forth to be a propitiation, through faith in his blood, to declare his righteousness: that he might be just, and the justifier of him which believeth in Jesus" (Rom 3:25, 26). "He that believeth shall be saved" (Mk 16:16). "As many as received him, to them gave he power to become the sons of God, even to them that believe on his name" (Jn 1:12).

"As Moses lifted up the serpent in the wilderness, even so must the Son of man be lifted up, that whosoever believeth in him should not perish but have eternal life; for God so loved the world, that he gave his only begotten Son, that whosoever believeth in him should not perish, but have everlasting life. He that believeth on him is not condemned: but he that believeth not is condemned already, because he hath not believed in the name of the only begotten Son of God" (Jn 3:14–18). "He that believeth on the Son hath everlasting life, and he that believeth not the Son shall not see life" (Jn 3:36). "He that heareth my word, and believeth on him that sent me, hath everlasting life" (Jn 5:24). "This is the work of God, that ye believe on him whom he hath sent" (Jn 6:29). "He that believeth on me shall never thirst" (Jn 6:35).

"This is the will of him that sent me, that every one which seeth the Son, and believeth on him, may have everlasting life" (Jn 6:40). "He that believeth in me, though he were dead, yet shall he live; and whosoever liveth and believeth in me shall never die" (Jn 11:25–26). "I am come a light into the world, that whosoever believeth on me should not abide in darkness" (Jn 12:46). "These are written that ye might believe that Jesus is the Christ, the Son of God, and that believing, ye might have life through his name" (Jn 20:31). "By him all that believe are justified from all things" (Acts 13:39). "Believe on the Lord Jesus Christ, and thou shalt be saved" (Acts 16:31). "To him give all the prophets witness, that through his name whosoever believeth in him shall receive remission of sins" (Acts 10:43). "To him that worketh not but believeth on him that justifieth the ungodly, his faith is counted for righteousness" (Rom 4:5). "Christ is the end of the law for righteousness to every one that believeth" (Rom

10:4). "If thou shalt confess with thy mouth the Lord Jesus, and shalt believe in thine heart that God hath raised him from the dead, thou shalt be saved" (Rom 10:9). "It pleased God by the foolishness of preaching to save them that believe" (1 Cor 1:21). "This is his commandment, that we should believe on the name of his Son Jesus Christ" (1 Jn 3:23). "We have known and believed the love that God hath to us" (1 Jn 4:16). "Whosoever believeth that Jesus is the Christ is born of God" (1 Jn 5:1). "He that believeth on the Son of God hath the witness in himself; he that believeth not God hath made him a liar, because he believeth not the record that God gave of his Son" (1 Jn 5:10). "He that believeth not shall be damned" (Mk 16:16).

These are some of the many texts which teach us what the link is between the sinner and the great salvation. They show that it is our belief of God's testimony concerning His own free love, and the work of His Son, that makes us partakers of the blessings which that testimony reveals. They do not ascribe any meritorious or saving virtue to our act of faith. They show us that it is the object of faith—the person, or thing, or truth of which faith lays hold—that is the soul's peace and consolation. But still they announce most solemnly the necessity of believing, and the greatness of the sin of unbelief.

In them God demands the immediate faith of all who hear His testimony. Yet He gives no countenance to the self-righteousness of those who are trying to perform the act of faith in order to qualify themselves for the favour of God; whose religion consists in performing acts of faith of a certain kind; whose comfort arises from thinking of these well-performed acts; and whose assurance comes from the summing up of these at certain times, and dwelling upon the superior quality of many of them.

In some places the word "trust" occurs where perhaps we might have expected "faith." But the reason of this is plain; the testimony which faith receives is testimony to a person and his good will, in which case belief of the testimony and confidence in the person are things inseparable. Our reception of God's testimony is confidence in God Himself, and in Jesus Christ His Son. Hence it is that Scripture speaks of "trust" or "confidence" as that which saves us, as if it would say to the sinner, "Such is the gracious character of God that you have only to put your case into His hands, however bad it be, and entrust your soul to His keeping, and you shall be saved."

In some places, we are said to be saved by the knowledge of God or of Christ; that is, by simply knowing God as He has made Himself known to us in Jesus Christ (Is 53:11; 1 Tm 2:4; 2 Pt 2:20). Thus Jesus spoke, "This is life eternal, that they might know thee, the only true God, and Jesus Christ whom thou hast sent" (Jn 17:3). And as if to make simplicity more simple, the apostle, in speaking of the facts of Christ's death, and burial, and resurrection, says, "By which ye are saved if ye keep in memory what I preached unto you" (1 Cor 15:1–2).

Thus God connects salvation with "believing," "trusting," "knowing," "remembering." Yet the salvation is not in our act of believing, trusting, knowing, or remembering; it is in the thing or person believed on, trusted, known, remembered. Nor is salvation given as a reward for believing and knowing. The things believed and known are our salvation. Nor are we saved or comforted by thinking about our act of believing, or ascertaining that it possesses all the proper ingredients and qualities which would induce God to approve of it, and of us because of it. This would be making faith a meritorious, or, at least, a qualifying work; and then grace would be no more grace. It would really be making our faith a part of Christ's work—the finishing stroke put to the great undertaking of the Son of God, which, otherwise, would have been incomplete, or, at least, unsuitable for the sinner as a sinner.

To the man that makes his faith and his trust his rest, and tries to pacify his conscience by getting up evidence of their solidity and excellence, we say, "miserable comforters are they all!" I get light by using my eyes; not by thinking about my use of them, nor by a scientific analysis of their component parts. So I get peace by and in believing; not by thinking about my faith, or trying to prove to myself how well I have performed the believing act. We might as well extract water from the desert sands as peace from our own act of faith. Believing in the Lord Jesus Christ will do everything for us; believing in our own faith, or trusting in our own trust, will do nothing.

Thus faith is the bond between us and the Son of God; and it is so, not because of anything in itself, but because it is only through the medium of truth, as known and believed, that the soul can get hold of things or persons.[1] Faith is nothing, save as it lays hold of Christ; and it does so by laying hold of the truth or testimony concerning Him. "Faith cometh by hearing, and hearing by the word of God," says the apostle. "Ye shall know the truth," says the Lord, "and the truth shall make you free" (Jn 8:32); and again, "Because I tell you the truth, ye believe me not. . . . And if I say the truth, why do ye not believe me?" (Jn 8:45–46).

We have also such expressions as these: "Those that know the truth" (1 Tm 4:3); "those that obey not the truth" (Rom 2:8); "as the truth is in Jesus" (Eph 4:21); "belief of the truth" (2 Th 2:13); "acknowledging of the truth" (2 Tm 2:25); "the way of truth" (2 Pt 2:2); "we are of the truth" (1 Jn 3:19); "sanctify them through thy truth" (Jn 17:17); "I speak forth the words of truth" (Acts 26:25); "the Spirit of truth will guide you into all truth" (Jn 16:13).

---

1. As a good memory means the power of correctly remembering the very things that have occurred, so the essence of a right faith is a belief of the right thing. And as a bad memory is refreshed or corrected by presenting again and again the objects to be remembered, so a wrong faith (or unbelief) requires to have the full testimony of God again and again presented to the soul.

In this matter there are (as in most Bible statements) two sides, both to be held fast: belief in a person, and belief of a truth. The former, carried to an exclusive excess, lands us in mysticism; the latter, carried to a like extreme, ends in rationalism. We must realise both the person and the truth.

Most memorable, in connection with this subject, are the Lord's warnings in the parable of the sower, especially the following: "The seed is the word of God. Those by the wayside are those that hear: then cometh the devil, and taketh away the word out of their hearts, lest they should believe and be saved" (Lk 8:11–12). The words, too, of the beloved disciple are no less so: "He that saw it bare record, and his record is true; and he knoweth that he saith true, that ye might believe" (Jn 19:35); and again, "These are written, that ye might believe that Jesus is the Christ, the Son of God; and that believing ye might have life through his name" (Jn 20:31).

This truth regarding Christ and His sacrificial work, the natural man hates, because he hates Christ Himself. "They hated me," says the Lord (Jn 15:25); even more, they hated me "without a cause" (Ps 69:4). It is not error that man hates, but truth; and hence the necessity for the Holy Spirit's work to remove that hatred; to make the sinner even so much as willing to know the truth or the True One. Yet there is no backwardness on the part of God to give the Spirit; and the first dawnings of inquiry and anxiety how that something beyond "flesh and blood" is at work in the soul.

But though it needs the power of the divine Spirit to make us believing men, this is not because faith is a mysterious thing, a great exercise or effort of soul, which must be very accurately gone through, in order to make it and us acceptable; but because of our dislike to the truth believed, and our enmity to the Being in whom we are asked to confide. Believing is the simplest of all mental processes; yet not the less is the power of God needed. Let not the inquirer mystify or magnify faith in order to give it merit or importance in itself, so that by its superior texture of quality it may justify him; yet never, on the other hand, let him try to simplify it, for the purpose of making the Spirit's work unnecessary. The more simple that he sees it to be, the more will he see his own guilt, in so deliberately refusing to believe, and his need of the divine Helper to overcome the fearful opposition of the natural heart to the simple reception of the truth.

The difficulty of believing has its real root in pure self-righteousness; and the struggles to believe, the endeavours to trust, of which men speak, are the indications and expressions of this self-righteousness. So far are these spiritual exercises from being tokens for good, they are often mere expressions of spiritual pride—evidences of the desperate strength of self-righteousness; the very earnestness of the struggle showing the intensity of the self-righteousness. It is worse than vain, then, to try to comfort an anxious soul by pointing to these efforts as proofs of existing faith. They are proofs either of ignorance or of unbelief—proofs of the sinner's determination to do anything rather than believe that all is done. Doubts are not the best evidence of faith; and attempts at performing this great thing called faith are more proofs of blindness to the finished propitiation of the Son of God.

To do some great thing called faith in order to win God's favour, the sinner has no objection; in fact, it is just what he wants, for it gives him the opportunity of working for his salvation. But he rejects the idea of taking his stand upon a work already done, and so ceasing his own efforts to effect a reconciliation, for which all that is needed was accomplished nineteen hundred years ago, upon the cross of Him who "was made sin for us, though he knew no sin; that we might be made the righteousness of God in him" (2 Cor 5:21).

9

Believe Just Now

You are in earnest now; but I fear you are making your earnestness your Christ, and actually using it as a reason for not trusting Christ *immediately*. You think your earnestness will lead on to faith, if it be but sufficiently intense, and long enough persisted in.

But there is such a thing as earnestness in the wrong direction: earnestness in unbelief, and a substitution of earnestness for simple faith in Jesus. You must not soothe the alarms of conscience by this earnestness of yours. It is unbelieving earnestness; and that will not do. What God demands is simple faith in the record which He has given you of His Son. You say, "I can't offer Him faith, but I can bring Him earnestness; and by giving Him earnestness, I hope to persuade Him to give me faith." This is self-righteousness. It shows that you regard both faith and earnestness as something to be done in order to please

God, and secure His good will. You say, "Faith is the gift of God, but earnestness is not; it is in my own power; therefore I will earnestly labour, and struggle, and pray, hoping that before long God will take pity on my earnest struggles." You even feel secretly that it would be hardly fair in Him to disregard such earnestness.

Now, if God has anywhere said that unbelieving earnestness or the unbelieving use of means is the way of procuring faith, I cannot object to such proceedings on your part. But I do not find that He has said so, or that the apostles, in dealing with inquirers, set them upon this preliminary process for acquiring faith. I find that the apostles shut up their hearers to immediate faith and repentance, bringing them face to face with the great object of faith, and commanding them in the name of the living God to believe, just as Jesus commanded the man with the withered hand to stretch it out. The Lord did not give him any directions as to a preliminary work, or preparatory efforts, and struggles, and using of means.

These are man's attempts to bridge over the great gulf of human appliances; man's way of evading the awful question of his own utter impotence, man's unscriptural devices for sliding out of inability into ability, out of unbelief into faith; man's plan for helping God to save him; man's self-made ladder for climbing up a little way out of the horrible pit, in the hope that God will so commiserate his earnest struggles, as to do all the rest that is needed.

Now God has commanded all men everywhere to repent; but He has nowhere given us any directions for obtaining repentance. God has commanded sinners to believe, but He has not prescribed for them any preparatory process, the undergoing of which will induce Him to give them something which He is not from the first most willing to do. It is thus that He shuts them up to faith by "concluding them in unbelief." It is thus that He brings them to feel both the greatness and the guilt of their inability; and so constrains them to give up every hope of doing anything to save themselves; driving them out of every refuge of lies, and showing them that these prolonged efforts of theirs are hindrances, not helps, and are just so many rejections of His own immediate help; so many distrustful attempts to persuade Him to do what He is already most willing to do in their behalf.

The great manifestation of self-righteousness is this struggle to believe. Believing is not a work, but a ceasing from work; and this struggle to believe is just the sinner's attempt to make a work out of that which is no work at all; to make a labour out of that which is a resting from labour. Sinners will not let go their hold of their former confidences and drop into Christ's arms. Why? Because they still trust these confidences, and do not trust Him who speaks to them in the gospel. Instead, therefore, of encouraging you to exert more and more earnestly these preliminary efforts, I tell you they are all the sad indications of self-righteousness. They take for granted that Christ has not done His work sufficiently, and that God is not willing to give you faith till you have plied Him with the arguments and importunities of months or years.

God is at this moment willing to bless you; and these struggles of yours are not, as you fancy, humble attempts on your part to take the blessing, but proud attempts either to put it from you, or to get hold of it in some way of your own. You cannot, with all your struggles, make the Holy Spirit more willing to give you faith than He is at this moment. But your self-righteousness rejects this precious truth; and if I were to encourage you in these "efforts," I should be fostering your self-righteousness and your rejection of this grace of the Spirit.

You say you cannot change your heart or do any good thing. So say I. But I say more. I say that you are not at all aware of the extent of your helplessness and of your guilt. These are far greater and far worse than you suppose. And it is your imperfect view of these that leads you to resort to these endeavours. You are not yet sensible of your weakness, in spite of all you say. It is this that is keeping you from God and God from you.

God commands you to believe and to repent. It is at your

peril that you attempt to alter this imperative and immediate obligation by the substitution of something preliminary, the performance of which may perhaps soothe your terrors, and lull your conscience to sleep, but will not avail either to propitiate God or to lift you into a safer or more salvable condition, as you imagine. For we are saved by faith, not by efforts to induce "an unwilling God" to give us faith. In going to God, we are to take for granted that He will fulfill His Word, and act according to His character. Our appeals are to be made, not to an unwilling, but to a willing God. We are not to try by our prayers or earnestness to persuade God to be gracious, to extort salvation from the hand of a grudging and austere giver. God is pressing His salvation upon us, and declaring His infinite willingness to bless at this moment.

God commands you to believe; and so long as you do not believe, you are making Him a liar, you are rejecting the truth, you are believing a lie; for unbelief is, in reality, the belief of a lie. Yes, God commands you to believe; and your not believing is your worst sin; and it is by exhibiting it as your worst sin that God shuts you up to faith. Now, if you try to extenuate this sin—if you flatter your soul that, by making all these earnest and laborious efforts to believe, you are lessening this awful sin, and rendering your unbelieving state a less guilty one—then you are deluding your conscience, and thrusting away from you that divine hand which, by this conviction of unbelief, is shutting you up to faith.

I do not remember having seen this better stated than in Fuller's *Gospel Worthy of All Acceptation*. I give a few sentences:

> It is the duty of ministers not only to exhort their carnal hearers to believe in Jesus Christ for the salvation of their souls; but it is at our peril to exhort them to anything short of it, or which does not involve or imply it. We have sunk into such a compromising way of dealing with the unconverted,

as to have well nigh lost sight of the spirit of the primitive preachers; and hence it is that sinners of every description can sit so quietly as they do in our places of worship. Christ and his apostles, without any hesitation, called on sinners to repent and believe the gospel; but we, considering them as poor, impotent, and depraved creatures, have been disposed to drop this part of the Christian ministry. Considering such things as beyond the power of their hearers, they seem to have contented themselves with pressing on them the things they *could* perform, still continuing enemies of Christ; such as behaving decently in society, reading the scriptures, and attending the means of grace.

Thus it is that hearers of this description sit at ease in our congregations. But as this implies no guilt on their part, they sit unconcerned, conceiving that all that is required of them is to lie in the way and wait the Lord's time. But is this the religion of the Scriptures? Where does it appear that the prophets or apostles treated that kind of inability, which is merely the effect of reigning aversion, as affording any excuse? And where have they descended in their exhortations to things which might be done, and the parties still continue the enemies of God? Instead of leaving out everything of a spiritual nature, because their hearers could not find it in their hearts to comply with it, it may be safely affirmed that they exhorted to nothing else, treating such inability not only as of no account with regard to the lessening of obligation, but as rendering the subjects of it worthy of the severest rebuke. . . .

Repentance toward God and faith towards our Lord Jesus Christ are allowed to be duties, but not immediate duties. The sinner is considered as unable to comply with them, and therefore they are not urged upon him; but instead of them, he is directed to pray for the Holy Spirit to enable him to repent and believe. This, it seems, he can do, notwithstanding the aversion of his heart from everything of the kind! But if any man be required to pray for the Holy Spirit, it must be either sincerely and in the name of Jesus, or insincerely and in some other way. The latter, I suppose, will be allowed to be an abomination in the sight of God; he cannot, therefore, be required to do this; and as to the former, it is just as difficult and as opposite to the carnal heart as repentance and faith themselves. Indeed, it amounts to the same thing; for a sincere desire after a spiritual blessing, presented in the name of Jesus, is no other than the prayer of faith.

The great thing which I would press upon your conscience is the awful guilt that there is in unbelief. Continuance in unbelief is continuance in the very worst of sins; and continuance in it because (as you say) you cannot help it is the worst aggravation of your sin. The habitual drunkard says he "cannot help it"; the habitual swearer says he "cannot help it"; the habitual unbeliever says he "cannot help it." Do you admit the drunkard's excuse? Or do you not tell him that it is the worst feature of his case, and that he ought to be utterly ashamed of himself for using such a plea? Do you say, "I know you can't give up your drunken habits, but you can go and pray to God to enable you to give up these habits, and perhaps God will hear you and enable you to do so"? What would this be but to tell him to go on drinking and praying alternately; and that, possibly, God may hear his drunken prayers, and give him sobriety? You would not thus deal with drunkenness, ought you to deal so with unbelief? Ought you not to press home its guilt; and to show a sinner that, when he says, "I can't help my unbelief," he is uttering his worst condemnation, and saying, "I can't help distrusting God, I can't help hating God, I can't help making God a liar"; and that he might just as well say, "I can't help stealing, and lying, and swearing"?

Never let unbelief be spoken of as a misfortune. It is awfully sinful. Its root is the desperate wickedness of the heart. How evil must that heart be when it will not even believe! If our helplessness and hardness of heart lessened our guilt, then the more wicked we became, we should be the less responsible and the less guilty. The sinner who loves sin so much that he "cannot" part with it is the most guilty. He who says, "I cannot love God," is proclaiming himself one of the worst of sinners; but he who says, "I cannot even believe," is taking to himself a guilt which we may truly call the darkest and most damnable of all.[1]

Oh, the unutterable guilt involved even in one moment's unbelief; one single act of an unbelieving soul! How much more is the continuous unbelief of twenty or sixty years! To steal once

---

[1]. There is a tendency among some to undervalue doctrine, to exalt morality at the expense of theology, and to deny the importance of a sound creed. I do not doubt that a sound creed has often covered an unsound life, and that "much creed, little faith," is true of multitudes. But when we hear it said, "Such a man is far gone in error, but his heart is in its right place; he disbelieves the substitution on the cross, but he rests on Christ himself," we wonder, and ask, What then was the Bible written for? It may be (if this be the case) a book of thought, but it is no standard of truth, no infallible expression of the mind of an infallible Being! The solemnity with which that book affirms the oneness of truth, and the awful severity with which it condemns every departure from the truth, as a direct attack on God Himself, show us the danger of saying that a man's heart may be in its right place though his head contains a creed of error.

Faith and unbelief are not mere mental manipulations to which no moral value is attached. Doctrine is not a mere form of thought or phase of opinion. Within what limits such might have been the case had there been no revelation, I do not say. But with a revelation, all mental transactions as to truth and error assume a moral character, with which the highest responsibility is connected; their results have a moral value, and are linked with consequences of the most momentous kind.

On true doctrine rests the worship of the true God. From error springs the worship of a false God. If, then, Jehovah is a jealous God, not giving His glory to another, unbelief must be one of the worst of sins; and error not only a deadly poison to the soul receiving it, but hateful to God, as blasphemy against Himself, and the same in nature as the blind theologies of paganism. The real root of all unbelief is atheism. Man's guilty conscience modifies this, turns it into idolatry; or his sentimental nature modifies it and turns it into pantheism. The fool's "No God" is really the root of all unbelief.

is bad enough. How much more to be a thief by habit and repute! We think it bad enough when a man is overtaken with drunkenness. How much more when we have to say of him, he is never sober. Such is our charge against the man who has not yet known Christ. He is a continuous unbeliever. His life is one unbroken course of unbelief, and hence of false worship, if he worships at all. Every new moment is a new act of unbelief; a new commission of the worst of sins; a sin in comparison with which all other sins both of heart and life, awful as they are, seem to lose their enormity. Let the thought of this guilt cut your conscience to the quick! Oh, tremble as you think of what it is to be, not for a day or an hour, but for a whole lifetime, an unbelieving man!

10

The Want of Power to Believe

You say, "I know all these things," yet they bring me no peace. I doubt much, in that case, whether you do know them; and I should like you to begin to doubt upon this point. You take for granted much too easily that you know them. Seeing they do not bring to your soul the peace which God says they are sure to do, your wisest way would be to suspect the correctness of your knowledge. If a trusted physician prescribes a sure medicine for some complaint, and if on trial I find that what I have taken does me no good, I begin to suspect that I have got some wrong medicine instead of that which he prescribed.

Now are you sure that the truth which you say you know is the very gospel of the grace of God? Or is it only something like it? And may not the reason of your getting no peace from that which you believe just be because it contains none? You have got hold of many of the good things, but you have missed, perhaps, the one thing which made it a "joyful sound." You believe perhaps the whole gospel save the one thing which makes it good news to a sinner. You see the cross as bringing salvation very near; but not so absolutely close as to be in actual contact with you as you are; not so entirely close but that there is a little space, just a handbreadth or a hairbreadth, to be made up by your own prayers, or efforts, or feelings. "Everything," you say, "is complete; but, then, that want of feeling in myself!" Ah, there it is! There is the little unfinished bit of Christ's work which you are trying to finish, or to persuade Him by your prayers to finish for you! That want of feeling is the little inch of distance which you have to get removed before the completeness of Christ's work is available for you!

The consciousness of insensibility, like the sense of guilt, ought to be one of your reasons for trusting Him the more, whereas you make it a reason for not trusting Him at all. Would a child treat a father or a mother thus? Would it make its bodily weakness a reason for distrusting parental love? Would it not feel that that weakness was thoroughly known to the parent, and was just the very thing that was drawing out more love and skill? A stronger child would need less care and tenderness. But the poor, helpless one would be of all others the most likely to be pitied and watched over. Deal thus with Christ, and make that hardness of heart an additional reason for trusting Him, and for prizing His finished work.

This state of mind shows that you are not believing the right thing, but something else, which will not heal your hurt; or, at least, that you are mixing up something with the right thing which will neutralise all its healing properties.

You must begin at the beginning once more; and go back to the simplest elements of heavenly truth, which are wrapped up in the great facts that "Jesus died and rose again"; facts too little understood, and undervalued by many; facts to which the apostles attached such vast importance, and on which they laid so much stress; facts out of which the early believers, without the delay of weeks or months, extracted their peace and joy.

You say, "I cannot believe." Let us look into this complaint of yours.

I know that the Holy Spirit is as indispensable to your believing, as is Christ in order to your being pardoned. The Holy Spirit's work is direct and powerful; and you will not rid yourself of your difficulties by trying to persuade yourself that His operations are all indirect, and merely those of a teacher presenting truth to you. Salvation *for* the sinner is Christ's work; salvation *in* the sinner is the Spirit's work. Of this internal salvation he is the beginner and the ender. He works in you in order to your believing, as truly as He works in you after you have believed, and in consequence of your believing.

This doctrine, instead of being a discouragement, is one of unspeakable encouragement to the sinner; and he will acknowledge this if he knows himself to be the thoroughly helpless being which the Bible says he is. If he is *not* totally depraved, he will feel the doctrine of the Spirit's work a hindrance, and an insult, no doubt, just as an able-bodied traveller would feel that you were both hindering and insulting him, if you were to tell him that he cannot set out on his journey without taking your arm. But as, in that case, he will be able to save himself without much assistance, he might just set aside the Spirit altogether, and work his way to heaven alone!

The truth is that without the Spirit's direct and almighty help, there could be no hope for a totally depraved being at all.

You speak of this inability to believe as if it were some unprovided-for difficulty; and as if the discovery of it had greatly cast you down. You would not have been so despondent had you found that you could believe of yourself without the Spirit; and it would greatly relieve you to be told that you could dispense with the Spirit's help in this matter. If this would relieve you, it is plain that you have no confidence in the Spirit; and you wish to have the power in your own hands because you believe your own willingness to be much greater than His. Did you but know the blessed truth, that His willingness far exceeds yours, you would rejoice that the power was in His hands rather than in your own. You would feel far more certain of attaining the end desired, when the strength needed is in hands so infinitely gracious; and you would feel that the man who told you that you had all the needed strength in yourself was casting down your best hope, and robbing you of a heavenly treasure.

How eagerly some grasp at the idea, that they *can* believe, and repent, and turn of themselves, as if it were consolation to the troubled spirit! As if this were the unraveling of its dark perplexities! Is it comfort to persuade yourself that you are not wholly without strength? Can you, by lessening the sum total of your depravity and inability, find the way to peace? Is it a relief to your burdened spirit to be delivered from the necessity of being wholly indebted to the Spirit of God for faith and repentance? Will it rescue you from the bitterness of despair to be told that, though you have not enough strength left to enable you to love God, yet in virtue of some little remaining power, you can perform this least of all religious acts, believing on the Son of God?

If such be your feeling, it is evident that you do not know the extent of your own disease, nor the depths of your evil heart; you don't understand the good news brought to you by the Son of God—of complete deliverance from all that oppresses you, whether it be guilt or helplessness. You have forgotten the blessed announcement, "In the LORD have I righteousness and *strength*" (Is 45:24). Your strength, as well as your righteousness, is in another; yet, while you admit the former, you deny the latter. You have forgotten, too, the apostle's rejoicing in the strength of his Lord; his feeling that when he was weak, then he was strong; and his determination to glory in his infirmities, that the power of Christ might rest upon him (2 Cor 12:9).

If you understand the genuine gospel in all its freeness, you will feel that the man who tries to persuade you that you have strength enough left to do without the Spirit is as great an enemy of the cross, and of your soul, as the man who wants to make you believe that you are not altogether guilty, but have some remaining goodness, and therefore do not need to be wholly indebted for pardon to the blood and righteousness of Immanuel.

"Without strength" is as literal a description of your state as "without goodness." If you understood the gospel, the consciousness of your total helplessness would just be the discovery that you are the very sinner to whom the great salvation is sent; that your inability was all foreseen and provided for, and that you are in the very position which needs, which calls for, and which shall receive, the aid of the almighty Spirit.

Till you feel yourself in this extremity of weakness, you are not in a condition (if I may say so) to receive the heavenly help. Your idea of remaining ability is the very thing that repels the help of the Spirit, just as any idea of remaining goodness thrusts away the propitiation of the Saviour. It is your not seeing that you have no strength that is keeping you from believing. So long as you think you have some strength, you will be trying to use that strength in *doing* something—and specially in performing, to your own and Satan's satisfaction, that great act or exercise of soul called "faith." But when you find out that you have no strength left, you will, in despair, cease to work—and (before you are aware)—believe! For, if believing be not a ceasing from work, it is at least the necessary and immediate result of it. You expended your little stock of imagined strength in holding fast the ropes of self-righteousness, but now, when the conviction of having no strength at all is forced upon you, you drop into the arms of Jesus. But this you will never do as long as you fancy that you have strength to believe.

Paul, after many years' believing, still drew his strength from Christ alone; how much more must you and others who have never yet believed at all? *He* said, "I take pleasure in my infirmities," that is, my want of strength. *You* say, "I am cast down because of it!"

They who tell you that you have some power left and that you are to use that power in believing and repenting are enemies of your peace, and subverters of the gospel. They in fact say to you that faith is a work, and that you are to do that work in order to be saved. They mock you. In yielding to them you are maintaining that posture which vexes and resists the Spirit who is striving within you; you are proudly asserting for fallen man a strength which belongs only to the unfallen; you are denying the completeness of the divine provision made for the sinner, in the fullness of Him in whom it pleased the Father that all fullness should dwell.

The following passage from an old writer is worth pondering:

> Ask him what it is he finds makes believing difficult to him. Is it unwillingness to be justified and saved? Is it unwillingness to be so saved by Jesus Christ to the praise of God's grace in him, and to the voiding of all boasting in himself? This he will surely deny. Is it a distrust of the truth of the gospel record? This he dare not own. Is it a doubt of Christ's ability or good-will to save? This is to contradict the testimony of God in the gospel. Is it because he doubts of an interest in Christ and his redemption? You tell him that believing on Christ makes up the interest in him. If he say that he cannot believe on Jesus Christ because of the difficulty of the acting this faith, and that a divine power is needful to draw it forth, which he finds not, you tell him that believing in Jesus Christ is no work, but a resting on Jesus Christ; and that this pretence is as unreasonable as that if a man wearied with a journey, and who is not able to go one step farther, should argue, "I am so tired that I am not able to lie down," when, indeed, he can neither stand nor go. The poor wearied sinner can never believe on Jesus Christ till he finds he can

do nothing for himself, and in his first believing doth always apply himself to Christ for salvation, as a man hopeless and helpless in himself. And by such reasonings with him from the gospel, the Lord will (as he has often done) convey faith, and joy, and peace, by believing.

Your puzzling yourself with this "cannot" shows that you are proceeding in a wrong direction. You are still labouring under the idea that this believing is a work to be done by you, and not the simple acknowledgment of a work done by another. You would do something in order to get peace, and you think that if you could only do this great thing called faith, God would reward you with peace. In this view, faith is a price as well as a work—whereas it is neither, but a ceasing from work and from attempting to pay for salvation. Faith is not a climbing of the mountain, but a ceasing to attempt it, and allowing Christ to carry you up in His arms.

You seem to think that it is your own act of faith that is to save you; whereas it is the object of your faith, without which your own act of faith, however well performed, is nothing. Supposing that this believing is a mighty work, you ask, "How am I to get it properly performed?" But your peace is not to come from any such performance, but entirely from Him to whom the Father is pointing, "Behold my servant whom I have chosen." As if He would say, "Look at Him as Israel looked at the serpent of brass: forget everything about yourself; your faith, your feelings, your repentance, your prayers; and look at Him." It is in Him, and not in your poor act of faith, that salvation lies. It is in Him and in His boundless love that you are to find your resting-place. It is out of Him, not out of your exercise of soul concerning Him, that peace is to come. Looking at your own faith will only minister to your self-righteousness.

To seek for satisfaction as to the quality or quantity of your faith, before you will take comfort from Christ's work, is to proceed upon the supposition that that work is not sufficient of itself to give you comfort as soon as received. That until made sufficient by a certain amount of religious feeling, it contains no comfort to the sinner. In short, that the comforting ingredient is an indescribable something, depending for its efficiency chiefly upon the superior excellence of your own act of faith, and the success of your own exertions in putting it forth.

Your inability, then, is not of performing aright this great act of believing, but of ceasing from all such self-righteous attempts to perform any act, or do anything whatever, in order to your being saved. So that the real truth is that you have not yet seen such a sufficiency in the one great work of the Son of God upon the cross, as to lead you utterly to discontinue your wretched efforts to work out something of your own. As soon as the Holy Spirit shows you the entire sufficiency of the great propitiation of the sinner, just as he is, you cease your attempts to act or work; and take, instead of all such exercises of yours, that which Christ has done. The Spirit's work is not to enable a man to do something which will save him or help to save him, but so to detach him from all his own exertions and performances, whether good, bad, or indifferent, that he shall be content with the salvation which the Saviour of the lost has finished.

Remember that what you call your inability, God calls your guilt, and that this inability is a wilful thing. It was not put into you by God, for He made you with the full power of doing everything He tells you to do. You disobey and disbelieve willingly. No one forces you to do either. Your rejection of Christ is the free and deliberate choice of your own will.

That inability of yours is a fearfully wicked thing. It is the summing up of your depravity. It makes you more like the devil than almost anything else. Incapable of loving God, or even of believing on His Son! Capable only of hating Him, and of rejecting Christ! O dreadful guilt! Unutterable wickedness of the human heart!

Is it really the "cannot" that is keeping you back from Christ? No; it is the "will not." You have not got the length of the "cannot." It is the "will not" that is the real and present barrier. "Ye *will not* come to me, that ye might have life" (Jn 5:40). "Whosoever *will*, let him take the water of life freely" (Rv 22:17).

If your heart would speak out, it would say, "Well, after all, I cannot, and God will not. I am doing all I can to believe, but the Spirit will not help me." And what is this but saying, "I have a hard-hearted God to deal with, who will not help or pity me." Whatever your rebellious heart may say, Christ's words are true, "Ye will not."

What He spoke, when weeping over impenitent Jerusalem, He speaks to you, "I *would*, but ye *would not*" (Mt 23:37). "They are fearful words," writes Dr. Owen, "'ye would not.' Whatever is pretended, it is will and stubbornness that lie at the bottom of this refusal." And oh! what must be the strength as well as the guilt of this unbelief, when nothing but the almightiness of the Holy Ghost can root it out of you!

You are perplexed by the doctrine of God's sovereignty and election.[1] I wonder that any man believing in a God should stumble at these. For if there be a God, a "King, eternal, immortal, and invisible," He cannot but be sovereign, and He cannot but do according to His own will, and choose according to His own purpose. You may dislike these doctrines, but you can only get rid of them by denying altogether the existence of an infinitely wise, glorious, and powerful Being. God would not be God were He not thus absolutely sovereign in His present doings and His eternal pre-arrangements.

---

1. Election has helped many a soul to heaven, but never yet hindered one. Depravity is the hindrance; election is God's way of overcoming that hindrance. And if that hindrance is not overcome in *all*, but only in *some*, who shall find fault? Was God bound to overcome it in all? Was he bound to bring every man to Christ, and to pluck every brand from the burning? Do not blame God for that which belongs solely to yourself, nor fret and be troubled about His sovereignty when the real root of the evil is your own desperately wicked heart.

But how would it solve your perplexities to get rid of sovereignty and election? Suppose these were set aside, you still remain the same depraved and helpless being as before. The truth is, that the sinner's real difficulty lies neither in sovereignty nor election, but in his own depravity. If the removal of these "hard doctrines" (as some call them) would lessen his own sinfulness, or make him more able to believe and repent, the hardship would lie at their door; but if not, then these doctrines are no hindrance at all. If it be God's sovereignty that is keeping him from coming to Christ, the sinner has serious matter of complaint against the doctrine. But if it be his own depravity, is it not foolish to be objecting to a truth that has never thrown one single straw of hindrance in the way of his return to God?[2]

---

2. Yet let me mention a way of speaking of this sovereignty which is not scriptural. Some tell the anxious sinner that the first thing he has to do, in order to faith, is to submit to this sovereignty, and that when he has done so, God will give him faith! This is far wrong, surely. Submission to the divine sovereignty is one of the highest results of faith; how can it be preparatory to faith? The sinner is told that he "cannot believe" of himself, but he can submit himself to God's sovereignty! He cannot do the lowest thing, but he can do the highest; and he must begin by doing the highest in order to prepare himself for doing the lowest! It is faith, not unbelief, that will thus submit; and yet the unconverted sinner is recommended to do, and to do in unbelief, the highest act of faith! This surely is turning theology upside down.

II

Insensibility

You say that you do not *feel* yourself to be a sinner; that you are not "anxious" enough; that you are not "penitent" enough.

Be it so. Let me, however, ask you such questions as the following:

1. *Does your want of feeling alter the gospel?* Does it make the good news less free, less suitable? Is it not glad tidings of God's love to the unworthy, the unlovable, the insensible?

2. *Is your want of feeling an excuse for your unbelief?* Faith does not spring out of feeling, but feeling out of faith. The less you feel, the more you should trust. You cannot feel aright till you have believed. As all true repentance has its root in faith, so all true feeling has the same. It is vain for you to attempt to reverse God's order of things.

3. *Is your want of feeling a reason for your staying away from*

Christ? A sense of want should lead you to Christ, and not keep you away. "More are drawn to Christ," says old Thomas Shepherd, "under a sense of a dead, blind heart, than by all sorrows, humiliations, and terrors." The less of feeling or conviction that you have, the more needy you are. And is that a reason for keeping aloof from Him? Instead of being less fit for coming, you are more fit. The blindness of Bartimeus was his reason for coming to Christ, not for staying away. If you have more blindness and deadness than others, you have so many more reasons for coming, so many fewer for standing far off. Whatever others may do who have convictions, you who have none dare not stay away, nor even wait an hour. You must come!

4. *Will your want of feeling make you less welcome to Christ?* How is this? What makes you think so? Has He said so, or did He act, when on earth, as if this were His rule of procedure? Had the woman of Sychar any feeling when He spoke to her so lovingly (Jn 4:10)? Was it the amount of conviction in Zaccheus that made the Lord address him so graciously: "Make haste, for today I must abide at thy house"? The balm will not be the less suitable for you, nor the physician the less affectionate and cordial, because, in addition to other diseases, you are afflicted with the benumbing palsy. Your greater need only gives Him an opportunity of showing the extent of His fullness, as well as the riches of His grace. Come to Him, then, just *because* you do not feel. "Him that cometh to me I will in no wise cast out." Whatever you may feel, or may not feel, it is still a faithful saying, and worthy of all acceptation, that Christ Jesus came into the world to save sinners. Do not limit the grace of God, nor suspect the love of Christ. Confidence in that grace and love will do everything for you; want of confidence, nothing. Christ wants you to come; not to wait, nor to stay away.

5. *Will your remaining away from Christ remove your want of feeling?* No. It will only make it worse; for it is a disease which He only can remove, so that a double necessity is laid upon you

for going to Him. Others who feel more than you may linger. You cannot afford to do so. You must go immediately to Him who is "a Prince and a Saviour, to give repentance to Israel, and the forgiveness of sins" (Acts 5:31). Seeing that distance and distrust will do nothing for you, try what "drawing near" and "confidence" will do. To you, though the chief of sinners, the message is, "Let us draw near" (Heb 10:22).

God commands you to come without any further delay or preparation; to bring with you your sins, your unbelief, your insensibility, your heart, your will, your whole man, and to put them into Christ's hands. God demands your immediate confidence and instant surrender to Christ. "Kiss the Son" is His message (Ps 2:12). His word insists on your return: "Return unto the LORD thy God" (Hos 14:1). It shows you that the real cause of the continuance of this distance is your unwillingness to let Christ save you in His own way, and a desire to have the credit of removing your insensibility by your own prayers and tears.

6. *Is not your insensibility one of your worst sins?* A hard-hearted child is one of the most hateful of beings. You may pity and excuse many things, but not hard-heartedness. Cease then to pity yourself, and learn only to condemn. Give this sin no quarter. Treat it, not as a misfortune, but as unmingled guiltiness. You may call it a disease; but remember that it is an inexcusable sin. It is one great all-pervading sin added to your innumerable others. This should shut you up to Christ. As an incurable leper, you must go to Him for cure. As a desperate criminal, you must go to Him for pardon. Do not, I beseech you, add to this awful sin the yet more damning sin of refusing to acknowledge Christ as the Healer of all diseases, and the Forgiver of all iniquities.

Repentance is only to be received from Christ. Why then should you make the want of it a reason for staying away from Him? Go to Him for it. He is exalted to give it. If you speak of "waiting," you only show that you are not sincere in your desire to have it. No man in such circumstances would think of waiting. Your conviction of sin is to come not by waiting, but by looking; looking to Him whom your sins have crucified, and whom by your distrust and unbelief you are crucifying afresh. It is written, "They shall look on me whom they have pierced, and they shall mourn" (Zec 12:10). It is not, they shall mourn and look, but they shall look and mourn.

Beware of fancying that convictions are to save you, or that they are to be desired for their own sakes. An old writer says, "Sense of a dead, hard heart is an effectual means to draw to Christ; yea, more effectual than any other can be, because it is the poor, the blind, the naked, the miserable, that are invited."

As to what is called a "law-work," preparatory to faith in Christ, let us consult the Acts of the Apostles. There we have the preaching of the apostolic gospel, and the fruits of it, in the conversion of thousands. We have several inspired sermons, addressed both to Jew and Gentile; but into none of these is the law introduced. That which pricked the hearts of the three thousand at Pentecost was a simple narrative of the life, death, burial, and resurrection of Jesus of Nazareth, concluding with these awful words, which must have sounded like the trumpet of doom to those who heard them, "Therefore let all the house of Israel know, that God hath made that same Jesus, whom ye have crucified, both Lord and Christ" (Acts 2:36). These were words more terrible than law; more overwhelming than Sinai heard. Awful as it would have been to be told, "You have broken the whole law of God"; it was not so awful as being told, "You have crucified His Son!" The sin of crucifying the Lord of glory was greater than that of breaking a thousand laws. And yet in that very deed of consummate wickedness was contained the gospel of the grace of God. That which pronounced the sinner's condemnation declared also his deliverance. There was life in that death; and the nails which fastened the Son of God to the cross, let out the pent-up stream of divine love upon the murderers themselves!

The gospel was the apostolic hammer for breaking hard hearts in pieces, for producing repentance unto life. It was a believed gospel that melted the obduracy of the self-righteous Jew; and nothing but the good news of God's free love, condemning the sin yet pardoning the sinner, will, in our own day, melt the heart of stone. "Law and terrors do but harden"; and their power, though wielded by an Elijah, is feeble in comparison with that of a preached cross.

The word "repentance" signifies in the Greek, "change of mind"; and this change the Holy Spirit produces in connection with the gospel, not the law. "Repent and believe the gospel" (Mk 1:15) does not mean, "get repentance by the law, and then believe the gospel"; but "let this good news about the kingdom which I am preaching lead you to change your views and receive the gospel." Repentance being put before faith here simply implies that there must be a turning from what is false in order to the reception of what is true. If I would turn my face to the north, I must turn it from the south; yet I should not think of calling the one of these preparatory to the other. If I want to get rid of the darkness, I must let in the light; but I should not say that the getting rid of the darkness is a preparation for receiving the light. These must, in the nature of things, go together. Repentance then is not, in any sense, a preliminary qualification for faith; least of all in the sense of sorrow for sin. "It must be reckoned a settled point," says Calvin, "that repentance not only immediately follows upon faith, but springs out of it. . . . They who think that repentance goes before faith, instead of flowing from or being produced by it, as fruit from a tree, have never understood its nature."[1] And Dr. Colquhoun remarks, "Saving faith is the mean of true repentance; and this repentance is not the mean but the end of that faith."[2]

---

1. *Institutes* 3.3.1.
2. *A View of Evangelical Repentance*. See the whole chapter on the Priority of Saving Faith to Repentance.

That terror of conscience may go before faith I do not doubt. But such terror is very unlike Bible repentance; and its tendency is to draw men away from, not to, the cross. That sinners may be awakened by the thunders of law I know. But these alarms are not godly sorrow. They are not uncommon among unbelieving men, such as Ahab and Judas. They will be heard with awful distinctness in hell; but they are not repentance. Sorrow for sin comes from "apprehension of the mercy of God in Christ," from the sight of the cross and of the love which the cross reveals. The broken and the contrite heart is the result of our believing the glad tidings of God's free love. In so far as repentance means sorrow for sin, or a change of mind respecting sin, it is produced only by looking to the cross. In so far as it is a change of mind in reference to God or Christ, it is the same with believing the gospel.

Few things are more dangerous to the anxious soul than the endeavours to get convictions, and terrors, and humiliations, as preliminaries to believing the gospel. They who would tell a sinner that the reason of his not finding peace is that he is not anxious enough, nor convicted enough, nor humbled enough, are enemies to the cross of Christ. They who would inculcate a course of prayer, and humiliation, and self-examination, and dealing with the law, in order to believing in Christ, are teaching what is the very essence of Popery; not the less poisonous and perilous because refined from Romish grossness, and administered under the name of gospel.

Christ asks no preparation of any kind whatsoever, legal or evangelical, outward or inward, in the coming sinner. And he that will not come as he is shall never be received at all. It is not "exercised souls," nor "penitent believers," nor "well-humbled seekers," nor earnest "users of the means," nor any of the better class of Adam's sons and daughters: but *sinners* that Christ welcomes. "He came not to call the righteous, but sinners to repentance" (Lk 5:32).

Spurious repentance, the product and expression of unbelief and self-righteousness, may be found previous to faith; just as all manner of evils abound in the soul before it believes. But when faith comes, it comes not as the result of this self-wrought repentance—but in spite of it; and this so-called repentance will be afterwards regarded by the believing soul as one of those self-righteous efforts, whose only tendency was to keep the sinner from the Saviour. They who call on "penitent sinners" to believe mistake both repentance and faith; and that which they teach is no glad tidings to the sinner. To the better class of sinners (if such there be) who have by laborious efforts got themselves sufficiently humbled, it may be glad tidings; but not to those who are "without strength," the lost, the ungodly, the hard-hearted, the insensible, the lame, the blind, the halt, the maimed.[3]

---

3. "It is not sound doctrine," says Dr. Colquhoun, "to teach that Christ will receive none but the true penitent, or that none else is warranted to come by faith to him for salvation. The evil of that doctrine is that it sets needy sinners on spinning repentance, as it were, out of their own bowels, and on bringing it with them to Christ, instead of coming to him by faith to receive it from him. If none be invited but the true penitent then impenitent sinners are not bound to come to Christ, and cannot be blamed for not coming." *A View of Evangelical Repentance.*

12

Jesus Only

You say, "I am not satisfied with the motives that have led me to seek Christ; they are selfish." That is very likely. The feelings of a newly awakened sinner are not disinterested, neither can they be so.

You have gone in quest of salvation from a sense of danger, or fear of the wrath to come, or a desire to obtain the inheritance of glory. These are some of the motives by which you are actuated. How could it be otherwise? God made you with these fears and hopes; and He appeals to them in His Word. When He says, "Turn ye, turn ye, for why will ye die?" He is appealing to your fears. When He sets eternal life before you, and the joys of an endless kingdom, He is appealing to your hopes. And when He presents these motives, He expects you to be moved by them. To act upon such motives, then, cannot be wrong. Indeed, not to act upon them would be to harden yourself against God's most solemn appeals. "Knowing therefore the terror of the Lord, we persuade men" (2 Cor 5:11), says Paul. It cannot be wrong to be influenced by this terror. "The remnant were affrighted, and gave glory to the God of heaven" (Rv 11:13). This surely was not wrong. The whole Bible is full of such motives, addressed to our hopes and fears.

When was it otherwise? Among the millions who have found life in Christ, who began in any other way, or started with a purely disinterested motive? Was it not thus that the jailor at Philippi began when the earthquake shook his soul and called up before his conscience the everlasting woe? Was it not a sense of danger and a dread of wrath that made him ask, "What shall I do to be saved?" And did the apostle rebuke him for this? Did he refuse to answer his anxious question because his motive was so selfish? No. He answered at once, "Believe on the Lord Jesus Christ, and thou shalt be saved."

There is nothing wrong in these motives. When my body is pained, it is not wrong to wish for relief. When overtaken by sickness, it is not wrong to send for a physician. You may call this selfishness, but it is a right and lawful selfishness, which He who made us what we are, and who gave us our instincts, expects us to act upon; and in acting on which, we may count upon His blessing, not His rebuke. It is not wrong to dread hell, to desire heaven, to flee from torments, to long for blessedness, to shun condemnation, and to desire pardon.[1] Let not Satan then

---

[1]. It is not wrong to love God for what He has done for us. Not to do so would be the very baseness of ingratitude. To love God purely for what He is, is by some spoken of as that highest kind of love, into which enters no element of self. It is not so. For in that case, you are actuated by the pleasure of loving; and this pleasure of loving an infinitely lovable and glorious Being of necessity introduces self. Besides, to say that we are to love God solely for what He is, and not for what He has done, is to make ingratitude an essential element of pure love. David's love showed itself in "not forgetting God's benefits" (Ps 103:2). But this so-called "pure love" soars beyond David's, and finds it a duty to be unthankful, lest perchance some selfish element mingles itself with its superhuman, superangelic purity.

ensnare you with such foolish thoughts, the tendency of which is to quench every serious desire, under the pretext of its not being disinterested and perfect.

You think that, if you were seeking salvation from a regard to the glory of God, you would be satisfied. But what does that mean, but that, at the very first, even before you have come to Christ, you are to be actuated by the highest of all motives? He who has learned to seek God's glory is one who has already come to Christ; and he who has learned to do this entirely, is no sinner at all; and, therefore, does not need Christ. To seek God's glory is a high attainment of faith; yet you want to be conscious of possessing it before you have got faith, indeed, in order to your getting it! Is it possible that you can be deluding yourself with the idea that if you could only secure this qualification, you might confidently expect God to give you faith? This would be substituting your own zeal for His glory, in the room of the cross of Christ.

Do not keep back from Christ under the idea that you must come to Him in a disinterested frame, and from an unselfish motive. If you were right in this thing, who could be saved? You are to come as you are, with all your bad motives, whatever these may be. Take all your bad motives, add them to the number of your sins, and bring them to the altar where the great sacrifice is lying. Go to the mercy seat. Tell the High Priest there, not what you desire to be, not what you ought to be, but what you are. Tell Him the honest truth as to your condition at this moment. Confess the impurity of your motives, all the evil that you feel or that you don't feel, your hard-heartedness, your blindness, your unteachableness. Confess everything without reserve. He wants you to come to Him exactly as you are, and not to cherish the vain thought that, by a little waiting, or working, or praying, you can make yourself fit, or persuade Him to make you fit.[2]

---

2. "How reasonable," writes one, "that we should just do that one small act which God requires of us—go and tell him the truth. I used to go and say,

"But I am not satisfied with my faith," you say. No, truly. Nor are you ever likely to be so. At least I should hope not. If you wait for this before you have peace, you will wait till life is done. It would appear that you want to believe in your own faith in order to obtain rest to your soul. The Bible does not say, "Being satisfied about our faith, we have peace with God," but "Being justified by faith, we have peace with God"; and between these two things there is a great difference.

Satisfaction with Jesus and His work, not satisfaction with your own faith, is what God expects of you. "I am satisfied with Christ," you say. Are you? Then you are a believing man; and what more do you wish? Is not satisfaction with Christ enough for you or for any sinner? And is not this the truest kind of faith? To be satisfied with Christ is faith in Christ. To be satisfied with His blood is faith in His blood. Do not bewilder yourself, nor allow others to bewilder you. Be assured that the very essence of faith is being satisfied with Christ and His sin-bearing work; ask no more questions about faith, but go on your way rejoicing, as one to whom Christ is all.

Remember the Baptist's words, "He must increase, but I must decrease" (Jn 3:30). Self, in every form, must decrease, and Christ must increase. To become satisfied with your faith would look as if you were dissatisfied with Christ. The beginning, the middle, and end of your course must be dissatisfaction with self and satisfaction with Christ. Be content to be satisfied with faith's glorious object, and let faith itself be forgotten. Faith, however

---

Lord, I am a sinner, do have mercy on me; but as I did not feel all this, I began to see that I was taking a lie in my hand, trying to persuade the Almighty that I felt things which I did not feel. These prayers and confessions brought me no comfort, no answer; so at last I changed my tone, and began to tell the truth—Lord, I do not feel myself a sinner; I do not feel that I need mercy. Now, all was right; the sweetest reception, the most loving encouragements, the most refreshing answers, this confession of the truth brought down from heaven. I did not get anything by declaring myself a sinner, for I felt it not; but I obtained everything by confessing that I did not see myself one."

perfect, has nothing to give you. It points you to Jesus. It bids you look away from itself to Him. It says, "Christ is all." It bids you look to Him who says, "Look unto me"; who says, "Fear not; I am the first and the last: I am he that liveth, and was dead; and, behold, I am alive for evermore" (Rv 1:17–18).

If you were required to believe in your own faith, to ascertain its quality, and to know that you are born again, before you were warranted to trust in Jesus, or to have peace, you would certainly need to be satisfied with your own faith. But you are not required to make good any personal claim, save that you are a sinner; not that you feel yourself to be one (that would open up an endless metaphysical inquiry into your own feelings); but simply that you are one. This you know upon God's authority, and learn from His Word; and on this you act, whether you feel your sinfulness or not. The gospel needs no ascertaining of anything about ourselves, save what is written in the Bible, and what is common to all Adam's children—that we need a Saviour. It is upon this need that faith acts; it is this need that faith presents at the throne of grace. The question, then, is not, Am I satisfied with my faith? But, Am I a needy sinner, and am I satisfied that in Christ there is all I need?

You say, "I am not satisfied with my love." What! Did you expect to be so? Is it your love to Christ, or His love to you, that is to bring you peace? God's free love to sinners, as such, is our resting place. There are two kinds of love in God—His love of compassion to the unbelieving sinner, and His love of delight and complacency to His believing children. A father's love to a prodigal child is quite as sincere as his love to his obedient, loving child at home, though it be of a different kind. God cannot love you *as a believer* till you are such. But He loves you as a poor sinner. And it is this love of His to the unloving and unlovable that affords the sinner his first resting place. This free love of God attracts and satisfies him. "Herein is love, not that we loved God, but that he loved us" (1 Jn 4:10). "We love him, because he first loved us" (1 Jn 4:19). "God so loved the world that he gave his only begotten Son" (Jn 3:16).

"I am not satisfied with my repentance," you say. It is well. What would you have thought of yourself had you been so? What pride and self-righteousness would it indicate were you saying, "I am satisfied with my repentance; it is of the proper quality and amount"? If satisfied with it, what would you do with it? Would you ground your peace upon it? Would you pacify your conscience with it? Would you go with it, instead of the blood, to a holy God? If not, what do you mean by the desire to be satisfied with repentance before having peace with God?

In short, you are not satisfied with any of your religious feelings, and it is well that you are not so; for, if you were, you must have a very high idea of yourself, and a very low idea of what both law and gospel expect of you. You are, no doubt, right in not being satisfied with the state of your feelings, but what has this to do with the great duty of immediately believing on the Son of God? If the gospel is nothing to you till you have got your feelings all set right, it is no gospel for the sinner at all. But this is its special fitness and glory, that it takes you up at the very point where you are at this moment, and brings you glad tidings in spite of your feelings being altogether wrong.

All these difficulties of yours have their root in the self-esteem of our natures, which makes us refuse to be counted altogether sinners, and which shrinks from going to God, save with some personal recommendation to make acceptance likely. Utter want of goodness is what we are slow to acknowledge. Give up these attempts to be satisfied with yourself in anything, great or small, faith, feeling, or action. The Holy Spirit's work in convincing you of sin is to make you dissatisfied with yourself, and will you pursue a course which can only grieve Him away? God can never be satisfied with you on account of any goodness about you; and why should you attempt to be satisfied with anything which will not satisfy Him?

There is but one thing with which He is entirely satisfied—the person and work of His only-begotten Son. It is with Him that He wants you to be satisfied, not with yourself. How much better would it be to take God's way at once, and be satisfied with Christ? Then would pardon and peace be given without delay. Then would the favour of God rest upon you. For God has declared that whoever is satisfied with Christ shall find favour with Him. His desire is that you should come to be at one with Him in this great thing. He asks nothing of you, save this. But with nothing else than this will He be content, nor will He receive you on any other footing, save that of one who has come to be satisfied with Christ, and with what Christ has done.

Surely all this is simple enough. Does it not exactly meet your case? Satisfaction with yourself, even if you could get it, would do nothing for you. Satisfaction with Christ would do everything; for Christ is all. "This is my beloved Son, in whom I am well pleased." Be pleased with Him in whom the Father is pleased, and all is well.

I suspect that some of those difficulties of yours arise from the secret idea that the gospel is just a sort of modified law, by keeping which you are to be saved. You know that the old law is far above your reach, and that it condemns, but cannot save you. But you think, perhaps, that Christ came to make the law easier, to lower its demands, to make it (as some say) an evangelical law, with milder terms, suited to the sinner's weakness. That this is blasphemy a moment's thought will show you. For it means that the former law was too strict; that is, it was not "holy, and just, and good." It denies also Christ's words, that He "came not to destroy but to fulfill the law." God has but one law, and it is perfect; its substance is love to God and man. A milder law must mean an imperfect one, a law that makes God's one law unnecessary, a law that gives countenance to sin. Will obedience to an imperfect law save a breaker of the perfect law? But faith does not make void the law; it establishes it (Rom 3:31).

It is by a perfect law that we are saved; else it would be an unholy salvation. It is by a perfect law, fulfilled in every "jot and tittle," that we are saved; else it would be an unrighteous salvation. The Son of God has kept the law for us; He has magnified it and made it honourable; and thus we have a holy and righteous salvation. Though above law in Himself, He was made "under the law" (Gal 4:4) for us; and by the vicarious law-keeping of His spotless life, as well as by endurance unto death of that law's awful penalties, we are redeemed from the curse of the law.

"Christ is the end [the fulfilling and exhausting] of the law for righteousness to every one that believeth" (Rom 10:4). For Christ is not a helper, but a Saviour. He has not come to enable us to save ourselves by keeping a mitigated law, but to keep the unmitigated law in our room, that the law might have no claim for penalty upon any sinner who will only consent to be indebted to the law-keeping and law-magnifying life and death of the divine Surety.

Other difficulties spring from confounding the work of the Spirit *in us* with that of Christ *for us*. These must be kept distinct; for the intermingling of them subverts both. Beware of overlooking either; or keeping them at a distance from each other. Though distinct, they go hand in hand, inseparably linked together; yet each having its own place and office. Your medicine and your physician are not the same, yet they go together. Christ is our medicine, the Spirit is your physician. Do not take the two works as if they were one compound work; nor build your peace upon some mystic gospel made up of a mixture of the two. Realise both, the outward and the inward, the objective and the subjective; Christ for us, the Holy Spirit in us.

As at the first, so to the last, this distinctiveness must be observed, lest, having found peace in believing, you lose it by not holding the beginning of your confidence steadfast to the end. "When I begin to doubt," writes one,

I quiet my doubts by going back to the place where I got them first quieted; I go and get peace again where I got it at the beginning; I do not sit down gloomily to muse over my own faith or unbelief, but over the finished work of Immanuel; I don't try to reckon up my experiences, to prove that I once was a believer, but I believe again as I did before; I don't examine the evidence of the Spirit's work in me, but I think of the sure evidences which I have of Christ's work for me in His death, and burial, and resurrection. This is the restoration of my peace. I had begun to look at other objects; I am now recalled from my wanderings to look at Jesus only.[3]

Some of your difficulties seem to arise from mixing up the natural and supernatural. Now the marvelous thing in conversion is that while all is supernatural (being the work of the Holy Ghost), all is also natural. You are, perhaps, expecting some miraculous descent of heavenly power and brightness into your

---

3. "Thus the poor and sorrowful soul, instead of being at once led to the source of all good, is taught to make much of the conflict of truth and falsehood within it as the pledge of God's love; and to picture to itself faith as a sort of passive quality, which sits amid the ruins of human nature, and keeps up what may be called a silent protest, or indulges a pensive meditation over its misery. And, indeed, faith thus regarded cannot do more, for while it acts, not to lead the soul to Christ, but to detain it from Him, how can the soul but remain a prisoner? True faith is what may be called colourless, like air or water; it is but the medium through which the soul sees Christ, and the soul as little rests on it and contemplates it as the eye can see the air. When men, then, are bent on holding it, as it were, in their hands, curiously inspecting, analysing, and so aiming at it, they are obliged to colour and thicken it, that it may be seen and touched. That is, they substitute for it something or other, a feeling, notion, sentiment, conviction, an act of reason, which they may hang over and dote upon. They rather aim at experiences within them, than at Him who is without them. Now men who are acted on by news, good and bad, or sights beautiful or fearful, admire, rejoice, weep, or are pained, but are moved spontaneously, not with a direct consciousness of their emotion. So is it with faith and other Christian graces. Bystanders see our minds, but our minds, if healthy, see but the objects which possess them."

soul; something apart from divine truth, and from the working of man's powers of mind. You have been expecting faith to descend, like an angel from heaven into your soul, and hope to be lighted up, like a new star in your firmament. It is not so.

The Spirit's work is beyond nature, but it is not against nature. He displaces no faculty; He disturbs no mental process; He does violence to no part of our moral framework; He creates no new organ of thought or feeling. His office is to "set all to rights" within you; so that you never feel so calm, so true, so real, so perfectly natural, so much yourself—as when He has taken possession of you in every part, and filled your whole man with His heavenly joy. Never do you feel so perfectly free—less constrained and less mechanical—in all your faculties, as when He has "brought into captivity every thought to the obedience of Christ." The heavenly life imparted is liberty, and peace; it is the removal of bondage, and darkness, and pain. So far from being a mechanical constraint, it is the removal of the iron chain with which guilt had bound us. It acts like an army of liberation to a downtrodden country, like the warm breath of spring to the frost-fettered tree. For the entrance of true life, or living truth, into man's soul must be liberty, not bondage. "The truth shall make you free."

Other difficulties arise out of confused ideas as to the proper order of truth. Misplaced truth is sometimes more injurious than actual error. In our statements of doctrine, we are to have regard to God's order of things, as well as to the things themselves. If you would solve the simplest question in arithmetic, the figures must not only be the proper ones, but they must be placed in proper order. So it is with the doctrines of the Word of God. Some seem to fling them about in ill-assorted couples, or confused bundles, as if it mattered little to the hearer or reader what order was preserved, provided only certain truths were distinctly announced. Much trouble to the anxious person has arisen from this reckless confusion.

A gospel in which election is placed first is not the gospel of the apostles, though certainly a gospel in which election is denied is still less the apostolic gospel. The true gospel is neither that Christ died for the elect, nor that He died for the whole world; for the excellency of the gospel does not lie in its announcement of the numbers to be saved, but in its proclamation of the great propitiation itself.

Some who are supposed to be holding fast "the form of sound words" present us with a mere dislocation of the gospel; the different truths being so jumbled, that while they may be all there, they produce no result. They so neutralise each other as to prevent the sinner extracting from them the good news which, when rightly put together, they most assuredly contain. If the verses of the Epistle to the Romans were transposed or jumbled together, would it be the Epistle to the Romans, though every word were there? So if, in teaching the gospel, we do not begin at the beginning—if, for instance, we tell the sinner what he has to do, before we tell him what God has done; if we tell him to examine his own heart before we tell him to study the cross of Christ—we take out the whole gladness from the glad tidings, and preach "another gospel."

Do we not often, too, study the Bible as if it were a book of law, and not the revelation of grace? We draw a cloud over it, and read it as a volume written by a hard master. A harsh tone is thus imparted to its words, and the legal element obscures the evangelical. We are slow to read it as a revelation of the love of the Father, Son, and Holy Ghost; as the book of grace, specially written for us by the Spirit of grace. The law no doubt is in it, yet the Bible is not law, but gospel. As Mount Sinai rears its head, an isolated mass of hard, red granite, amid a thousand desert mountains of softer and less stern material, so does the law stand in the Bible—a necessary part of it—but not the characteristic of it; "added because of transgressions, till the seed should come" (Gal 3:19). Yet have not our suspicious hearts darkened this Book of light? Do we not often read it as the proclamation of a command *to do*, instead of a declaration of what the love of God has done?

In going to God at first, are you to take for granted His willingness or His unwillingness to bless? Most seem to do the latter. They even defend themselves by saying that if they knew they were converted, they would take His willingness for granted, but not being sure of this they dare not do so! As if the gospel were not the revelation of His willingness to receive sinners as such!

How strange! We believe in Satan's willingness to tempt and to injure, but not in God's willingness to deliver and to save! We yield to our great enemy when he seduces into sin, and leads away from Christ and heaven, but we will not yield to our truest Friend when He draws us with the bands of love! We will not give God credit for speaking truly when He speaks in tender mercy, and utters over the sinner the yearnings of His unfathomable pity. We listen as if His words were hollow, as if He did not mean what He says, as if His messages of grace, instead of being the most thoroughly sincere that ever fell on human ears, were mere words spoken as a matter of course.

There is nothing in the whole Bible to repel the sinner, and yet the sinner will not come! There is everything to draw and to win, yet the sinner stands aloof! Christ receives sinners, yet the sinner turns away! He yearns over them, weeps over them, as over Jerusalem; yet the sinner is unmoved! The heavenly compassion is unavailing; the infinite long-suffering does not touch the stony heart, and the divine tears are thrown away. The Son of God stretches out His hands all the day long, but the outstretched hands are disregarded. All, all seems in vain to arrest the heedless, and to win back the wanderer.

Oh! the amount of divine love that has been expended upon this sad world; that has been brought to bear upon the needy sons of men! We sometimes almost doubt whether it be true or possible that God should lavish such love on such a world. But the cross is the precious memorial of the love, and that saying stands unchangeable: "God so loved the world, that he gave his only begotten Son." Sometimes, too, we say, "What is the use of throwing away such love? Is not the earnestness of God disproportioned to the littleness of its object—man?" It would be so were this life all; were there no eternity, no heaven, no hell, no endless gladness, and no everlasting woe. But with such a destiny as man's, with an eternity like that which is in store for him, can any amount of earnestness be too great? Can love or pity exceed their bounds? Can the joy or grief over a sinner saved or lost be exaggerated?

He whose infinite mind knows what heaven is, knows what its loss must be to an immortal being. Can He be too much in earnest about its gain? He whose all-reaching foresight knows what hell is, in all its never-ending anguish, sees far off and fathoms the horrors of the lost soul, its weeping and wailing and gnashing of teeth for ever and for ever, its horrible sense of condemnation and unmitigated woe, its cutting remorse, its too-late repentance, its hopeless sighs, its bitter memories of earth's sunny hours; with all the thousand sadnesses that go to make up the sum total of a lost eternity! Can He then pity too much? Can He yearn too tenderly over souls that are madly bent on flinging themselves into a doom like this? Can He use words too strong or too affectionate, in warning them against such a darkness and such a devil, and such a hell; in beseeching them to make sure of such a heaven as His?

In the minds of some, the idea prevails that sin quenches pity for the sinner in the heart of God. It is not so. That it shall do so hereafter, and that God will cease to pity the lost, is an awful truth. The lost soul's eternity will be an unpitied eternity of woe. But, meanwhile, God's hatred of the sin is not hatred of the sinner. Nay, the greatness of his sin seems rather to deepen than to lessen the divine compassion. At least we may say that the increasing misery which increasing sin entails calls into new intensity the paternal pity of "the God of the spirits of all flesh." "It grieves him at his heart" (Gn 6:6). The further the prodigal goes into the far country, the more do the yearnings of the father's heart go out after him, in unfeigned compassion for the wretched wanderer, in his famine, and nakedness, and degradation, and hopeless grief.

No; sin does not quench the pitying love of God. The kindest words ever spoken to Israel were in the very height of their apostasy. The most gracious invitation ever uttered by the Lord was to Capernaum, and Bethsaida, and Chorazin, "Come unto me." The most loving message ever sent to a church was that to Laodicea, the worst of all the seven, "Behold, I stand at the door, and knock." It was Jerusalem, in her extremity of guilt and unbelief, that drew forth the tears of the Son of God. No, sin does not extinguish the love of God to the sinner. Many waters cannot quench it, nor can the floods drown it. From first to last, God pursues the sinner as he flies from Him; pursues him not in hatred but in love; pursues him not to destroy, but to save.

God is not a man that He should lie. He means what He says when He speaks in pity, as truly as when He speaks in wrath. His words are not, like man's, random expressions or utterances of vague sentiment or highly wrought representations of feelings. His words are all true and real. You cannot exaggerate the genuine feeling which they contain; and to understand them as figures is not only to convert them into unrealities, but to treat them as falsehoods. Let sinners take God's words as they are; the genuine expressions of the mind of that infinitely truthful Being, who uses nothing but the words of "truth and soberness."

He is sovereign; but that sovereignty is not at war with grace; nor does it lead to insincerity of speech, as some seem to think. Whether we can reconcile the sovereignty with the pity, it does not matter. Let us believe them both, because both are revealed. Nor let us resort to an explanation of the words of pity which would imply that they were not sincerely spoken, and that if a sinner took them too literally and too simply, he would be sorely disappointed, finding them at last delusive exaggerations, if not empty air.

When Christ was on earth, He received and blessed and healed every one who came to Him. Divine sovereignty did not hamper divine love, nor did love interfere with sovereignty. Each had its own place. There was no conflict between them. Christ spoke truly when He said, "No man can come unto me except the Father draw him"; and He spoke as truly when He said, "Him that cometh to me I will in no wise cast out."

Let us learn to treat God as not merely the holiest, but the most truthful of all beings. Let the heedless sinner hear His truthful warnings, and tremble, for they shall all be fulfilled. Let the anxious sinner listen to His truthful words of grace, and be at peace. We need to be told this. For there is in the minds of many a feeling of sad suspicion as to the sincerity of the divine utterances, and a tendency to evade their honest meaning; and this even among those who do not seem at all aware of such distrust. Let us do justice to the truthfulness of God.

God is love. Yes, God is love. Can such a God be suspected of insincerity in the declarations of His long-suffering, in His words of yearning compassion toward the most rebellious and impenitent of men? That there is such a thing as righteousness, that there is such a place as hell, that there are such beings as lost angels and lost men, we know to be awful certainties. But however terrible, and however true, these things may be, they cannot cast the slightest doubt upon the sincerity of the great oath which God has sworn before heaven and earth, that He has "no pleasure in the death of the wicked"; nor in the least blunt the solemn edge of His gracious entreaty, "Turn ye, turn ye, for why will ye die?"

God's Way of
HOLINESS

Preface

The way of peace and the way of holiness lie side by side, or rather, they are one. That which bestows the one imparts the other, and he who takes the one takes the other also. The Spirit of peace is the Spirit of holiness. The God of peace is the God of holiness.

If at any time these paths seem to separate, there must be something wrong—wrong in the teaching that makes them seem to part company, or wrong in the state of the man in whose life they have done so.

They start together, or at least so nearly together that no eye, save the divine, can mark a difference. Yet, properly speaking, the peace goes before the holiness, and is its parent. This is what divines call "priority in nature, though not in time," which means substantially this: that the difference in such almost identical beginnings is too small in point of time to be perceived by us, yet it is not on that account the less distinct and real.

The two are not independent. There is fellowship between them, vital fellowship, each being the helpmeet of the other. The fellowship is not of mere coincidence, as in the case of strangers who happen to meet on the same path, nor of arbitrary appointment, as in the case of two parallel roads, but of mutual help and sympathy—like the fellowship of head and heart, or of two members of one body, the peace being indispensable to the production or causation of the holiness, and the holiness indispensable to the maintaining and deepening of the peace.

He who affirms that he has peace, while living in sin, is "a liar, and the truth is not in him." He who thinks that he has holiness, though he has no peace, ought to question whether he understands aright what the Bible means by either the one or the other; for, as the essence of holiness is the soul's right state toward God, it does not seem possible that a man can be holy so long as there is no conscious reconciliation between God and him. A spurious holiness there may be, founded upon a spurious peace, or upon no peace at all; but true holiness must start from a true and authentic peace.

Horatius Bonar
Kelso, Scotland
July 1864

I

The New Life

It is to a new life that God is calling us; not to some new steps in life, some new habits or ways or motives or prospects, but to a new life.

For the production of this new life the eternal Son of God took flesh, died, was buried, and rose again. It was not life producing life, a lower life rising into a higher, but life rooting itself in its opposite, life wrought out of death, by the death of "the Prince of life." Of the new creation, as of the old, He is the author.

For the working out of this, the Holy Spirit came down in power, entering men's souls and dwelling there, that out of the old He might bring forth the new.

That which God calls new must be so indeed. For the Bible means what it says, as being, of all books, not only the most true in thought, but the most accurate in speech. Great, then, and authentic must be that "new thing in the earth" which God "creates," to which He calls us, and which He brings about by such stupendous means and at such a cost. Most hateful also must that old life of ours be to Him, when, in order to abolish it, He delivers up His Son; and most dear must we be in His sight when, in order to rescue us from the old life, and make us partakers of the new, He brings forth all the divine resources of love and power and wisdom, to meet the exigencies of a case which would otherwise have been wholly desperate.

The man from whom the old life has gone out, and into whom the new life has come, is still the same individual. The same being that was once "under law" is now "under grace." His features and limbs are still the same; his intellect, imagination, capacities, and responsibilities are still the same. But yet old things have passed away; all things have become new. The old man is slain; the new man lives. It is not merely the old life retouched and made more comely, defects struck out, roughnesses smoothed down, graces stuck on here and there. It is not a broken column repaired, a soiled picture cleaned, a defaced inscription filled up, an unswept temple whitewashed. It is more than all this—otherwise, God would not call it a new creation, nor would the Lord have affirmed with such awful explicitness, as He does in His conference with Nicodemus, the divine law of exclusion from and entrance into the kingdom of God (Jn 3:3). Yet how few in our day believe that "that which is born of the flesh is flesh; and that which is born of the Spirit is spirit" (Jn 3:6).

Hear how God speaks! He calls us "newborn babes" (1 Pt 2:2), "new creatures" (Gal 6:15), a "new lump" (1 Cor 5:9), a "new man" (Eph 2:15), doers of "a new commandment" (1 Jn 2:8), heirs of "a new name" and a new city (Rv 2:17; 3:12), expectants of "new heavens and a new earth" (2 Pt 3:13). This new being, having begun in a new birth, unfolds itself in "newness of spirit" (Rom 7:6), according to a "new covenant" (Heb 8:8), walks along a "new and living way" (Heb 10:20), and ends in the "new song" and the "new Jerusalem" (Rv 5:9; 21:2).

It is no outer thing, made up of showy moralities and benevolences, or picturesque rites and graceful routine of devotion, or sentimentalisms bright or somber, or religious utterances on fit occasions, as to the grandeur of antiquity, or sacramental grace, or the greatness of creaturehood, or the nobleness of humanity, or the universal fatherhood of God. It is something deeper, and truer, and more genial, than that which is called deep, and true, and genial in modern religious philosophy. Its affinities are with the things above; its sympathies are divine; it sides with God in everything; it has nothing, beyond a few expressions, in common with the superficialities and falsehoods which, under the name of religion, are current among multitudes who call Christ "Lord" and "Master."

A Christian is one who has been "crucified with Christ," who has died with Him, been buried with Him, risen with Him, ascended with Him, and is seated "in heavenly places" with Him (Rom 6:3–8; Gal 2:20; Eph 2:5,6; Col 3:1–3). As such, he reckons himself dead unto sin, but alive unto God (Rom 6:11). As such, he does not yield his members as instruments of unrighteousness unto sin, but he yields himself unto God, as alive from the dead, and his members as instruments of righteousness unto God. As such, he seeks "the things which are above," and sets his affection on things above, mortifying his "members which are upon the earth; fornication, uncleanness, inordinate affection, evil concupiscence and covetousness, which is idolatry" (Col 3:1–5).

This newness is comprehensive, both in its exclusion of the evil and its inclusion of the good. It is summed up by the apostle in two things: righteousness and holiness. "Put off," says he, "the old man, which is corrupt, according to the deceitful lusts; and be renewed in the spirit of your mind; . . . put on the new man, which after God is created in righteousness and true holiness" (Eph 4:22–24), literally "righteousness and holiness of the truth," that is, resting on the truth. The new man, then, is meant to be righteous and holy, inwardly and outwardly, before God and man, as respects law and gospel, and this through the truth. For as that which is false ("the lie," v. 25) can only produce unrighteousness and unholiness, so the truth produces righteousness and holiness through the power of the Holy Ghost. Error injures, truth heals; error is the root of sin, truth is that of purity and perfection.

It is, then, to a new standing or state, a new moral character, a new life, a new joy, a new work, a new hope, that we are called. He who thinks that religion comprises anything less than this knows nothing yet as he ought to know. For that which man calls "piety," less may suffice; but the divine recognition can be accorded to no religion which does not in some degree embrace these.

These are weighty words of the apostle: "We are His workmanship."[1] Of Him, and through Him, and to Him are all things pertaining to us. Chosen, called, quickened, washed, sanctified, and justified by God Himself, we are in no sense our own deliverers. The quarry out of which the marble comes is His; the marble itself is His, the digging and hewing and polishing are His; He is the sculptor and we the statue.

"We are His workmanship," says the apostle. But this is not all. We are, he adds, "created in Christ Jesus unto good works, which God hath before ordained that we should walk in them." The plan, the selection of the materials, the model, the workman, the workmanship, are all divine; and though it doth not yet appear what we shall be, we know that we shall be "like Him," His image reproduced in us, Himself represented by us, for we are "renewed in knowledge after the image of Him that created us" (Col 3:10).

---

1. "His poem," the production of His wisdom, love, and power; that which He and only He can make (Eph 2:10). A house should be worthy of the builder, and a poem of him from whom it comes (Ps 100:3).

It is not, however, dead, cold marble that is to be wrought upon. That is simple work, requiring just a given amount of skill. But the remolding of the soul is unspeakably more difficult, and requires far more complex appliances. The influences at work in opposing—internal and external, spiritual, legal, physical—are many; and equally numerous must be the influences brought into play to meet all these, and carry out the design. The work is not mechanical, but moral and spiritual (physical in a sense, as dealing with the nature of things, but more truly, moral and spiritual). Omnipotence is not mere unlimited physical power, operating, as upon inanimate matter, by mere intensity of volition; but power which, with unlimited resources at its command, exhibits its greatness by regulating its flows according to moral circumstances. It produces its greatest results by indirect moral influences, developing itself on the one hand in conformity with law and sovereignty, and holy love, and on the other with human guilt, creature responsibility, and free volition. The complexities thus introduced are infinite, and the "variable quantities," if one may so speak, are so peculiar and so innumerable that we can find no formula to help us in the solution of the problem. We get bewildered in speculating on the processes by which omnipotence deals with moral beings, either in their sinfulness or their holiness.

Here let us also notice the duality or twofoldness of divine truth, the overlooking of which has occasioned much fruitless controversy and originated many falsehoods. Truth is, indeed, not two sided, but many sided, like a well-cut crystal. In a more general sense, however, it is truly double, with a heavenly and an earthly, a divine and a human side or aspect. It is at the line where these two meet that the greatest nicety of adjustment is required, and hence it is here that divergent theologies have come specially into conflict. The heavenward and the earthward aspects of truth must be carefully distinguished—the one fitting into the other, the one the counterpart of the other. God is absolute Sovereign; this is the one side. Man has volition of his own, and is not a machine or a stone; that is the other. God chooses and draws according to the good pleasure of His will, yet he hinders no man from coming or from willing. God is the giver of faith, yet "faith cometh by hearing, and hearing by the Word of God" (Rom 10:17). Hence, the difficulty of believing is not from the absence of proper faculties, but from the derangement of these, and conversion is God's restoration of these to their original nature. Faith is not a foreign gem imported into the soul, distinct from all our original powers; it is simply the man believing, in consequence of his soul being set right by the Holy Spirit—but he believes and disbelieves in the same way as before. It is not the intellect, or the mind, or the affections, that believe; it is the man, the whole man, the same whole man that formerly disbelieved. Very absurd and unphilosophical (not to mention unscriptural) have been the questions raised as to the seat of faith: whether it is in the intellect, or the will, or the heart. Faith is the man believing, just as love is the man loving. In Romans 10:9, the apostle is not contrasting the heart with the mind, but with the mouth—in other words, the inner with the outer man.

God works in us both to will and to do, yet He commands us to work out our salvation with fear and trembling. It is God that sanctifies us, yet it is through "the truth" that we are sanctified (Jn 17:17). It is God that purifies (Ti 2:14), yet it is by faith that our hearts are purified (Acts 15:9). It is God that fills us with joy and peace, and yet this is "in believing." This duality is the key to the solution of many a hard controversy. The movements of man's intellect are not superseded by God but assumed and regulated; the intellect itself is not overborne and forced, but set free to work its true work truly.[2] The "heavenly things" and

---

2. The more thoroughly we can study the Word of God, the better; and all critical helps are to be welcomed. Genuine scholarship, consecrated to the

"earthly things" are distinct, yet not separate; always to be viewed in connection with each other, yet not confused; for confusion here is mysticism, superstition, and false doctrine. "There are celestial bodies, and bodies terrestrial; but the glory of the celestial is one, and the glory of the terrestrial is another" (1 Cor 15:40). In every Bible truth there are two elements, the divine and the human; but the divine element is one thing, the human another. The theology that embodies most truth is that which knows how to recognise both of these, without confusion, yet without isolation or antagonism, and which refuses to merge either the divine in the human or the human in the divine.³

Hence the necessity for confining ourselves to the Word, and the danger of introducing human metaphysics into questions connected with the spiritual change wrought on us. It is God that works; it is we who are wrought upon; and everything needful to be known in connection with this work is revealed in the divine record. We give this thought some prominence because of the tendency with many to magnify humanity, and to undervalue the greatness of that change which begins the Christian course and character. No elevation of natural taste, no infusion of religious or benevolent earnestness, no cultivation of the intellect, can fill up the description given us in the word of one "who fears God," and is "called according to His purpose," "begotten again

---

elucidation of the Word, is an accomplishment of no common price. Everything that brings our souls into full contact with "the Word," in its fullness and variety, so as to steep them in it, is to be greatly prized, as fitted to make us holier, more fruitful, and more spiritual men.

3. We hear much of the divine and the human element in Scripture; nor is the expression amiss; yet might we not rather say that the Bible is all human and yet all divine? It is perfect according to what God meant it to be, though we may note what we call "imperfections" in it. The mountains of earth, in their ruggedness, are perfect in their way, though they have not the artificial perfection of the statue or the temple. God has chosen that His book and His world should resemble each other in that kind of perfection—a perfection which man appreciates in the landscape, but depreciates in the Bible.

unto a lively hope by the resurrection of Jesus Christ from the dead" (1 Pt 1:3). And we urge this the more decidedly because, as is the beginning, so will be the middle and the end. A false idea or a diverging step at the outset may lead to a false religion throughout life, to an imperfect and superficial goodness, as one incorrect figure or sign in an equation falsifies both process and result. If the dislocated joint is not properly set, it will never work comfortably; and if the wound is merely skinned over, the disease may be taking its own way underneath, all the more fatally because it is supposed to have been removed.

How the Holy Spirit operates in producing the newness of which we have spoken, we know not; yet we know that He does not destroy or reverse man's faculties. He renovates them all, so that they fulfill the true ends for which they were given. As He does not make the hand the foot, nor the eye the ear, so He does not make the heart the intellect, nor the will the judgment. Each faculty remains the same in end and use as before, only purified and set properly to work. Nor does the Holy Spirit supersede the use of our faculties by His indwelling. Rather, this indwelling makes these more serviceable, more energetic, each one doing its proper work and fulfilling its proper office; while the whole man, body, soul and spirit, instead of being brought under mechanical constraint, is made more truly free, never more fully himself than when filled with the Holy Spirit. For the result of the indwelling Spirit is liberty, not bondage, nor the production of an artificial character.

Thus, although no violence is done to our being in regeneration, omnipotence is at work at every point. Our new being is not the result of a mechanical process, yet it is the product of divine power. God claims it as a "creation," and as His own handiwork. "He that hath wrought us for the selfsame thing is God" (2 Cor 5:5), where the word implies the thorough elaboration of some difficult piece of work. "It is God which worketh in [us] both to will and to do of His good pleasure" (Phil 2:13), where the expressions indicate an operation which influences our "willing" as well as our "doing," and this on account of His being "well pleased" with Christ (Mt 3:17) and with His own eternal design. "God's tillage" (or husbandry, 1 Cor 3:9) is His name for us when speaking as a husbandman; "God's building" (or fabric) is His name when speaking as an architect. It is to the image of His Son that He has predestinated us to be conformed, that He might be the firstborn among many brethren (Rom 8:29), having "chosen us in Him before the foundation of the world, that we should be holy and without blame before Him in love" (Eph 1:4).

It is, then, to holiness that God is calling us (1 Th 4:7); that we should have our "fruit unto holiness" (Rom 6:22); that our hearts should be established "unblameable in holiness" (1 Th 3:13); that we should abound in "all holy conversation and godliness" (2 Pt 3:11); that we should be "a holy priesthood" (1 Pt 2:5), "holy in all manner of conversation" (1 Pt 1:15), "called with a holy calling" (2 Tm 1:9), "holy and without blame before Him in love" (Eph 1:4), presenting not only our souls but also our bodies as (not only a living but also) a holy sacrifice to God (Rom 12:1); indeed, remembering that these bodies are not only "a sacrifice," but a "temple of the Holy Ghost" (1 Cor 6:19).

Holiness is likeness to God, to Him who is the Holy One of Israel, to Him whom they laud in heaven as "Holy, holy, holy" (Rv 4:8). It is likeness to Christ, to "that Holy Thing" which was born of the virgin, to Him who was "holy, harmless, undefiled, separate from sinners" (Heb 7:26). It is not only disjunction from evil, and from an evil world; but it is also separation unto God and His service. It is priestly separation, for priestly service. It is distinctiveness such as that which marked the tabernacle and all its vessels, separation from every common use: separation by blood, "the blood of the everlasting covenant," this blood (or that which it signifies, namely, death) being interposed between us and all common things, so that we are dead to sin, but alive unto God, alive to righteousness, having died and risen in Him whose blood has made us what we are: saints, holy ones.

This holiness or consecration extends to every part of our persons, fills up our being, spreads over our life, influences everything we are, or do, or think, or speak, or plan, small or great, outward or inward, negative or positive, our loving, our hating, our sorrowing, our rejoicing, our recreations, our business, our friendships, our relationships, our silence, our speech, our reading, our writing, our going out and our coming in—in other words, our whole man in every movement of spirit, soul, and body. In the house, the sanctuary, the chamber, the market, the shop, the desk, the highway, it must be seen that ours is a consecrated life.

In one aspect, sanctification is an act, a thing done at once, like justification. The moment the blood touches us—that is, as soon as we believe God's testimony to the blood—we are "clean" (Jn 15:3), "sanctified," set apart for God. It is in this ceremonial or priestly sense that the word is used in the Epistle to the Hebrews; for as that to the Romans takes us into the forum and deals with our legal standing, so that to the Hebrews takes us into the temple, and deals with our priestly standing. As the vessels of the sanctuary were at once separated to God and His service, the moment the blood touched them, so are we. This did not imply that those vessels required no daily cleansing afterwards, and so neither does our consecration imply that we need no daily sanctifying, no inward process for getting rid of sin. The initiatory consecration through the blood is one thing, and the continual sanctifying by the power of the Holy Ghost is another. The former is the first step, the introduction to the latter—indeed, absolutely indispensable to any progress in the latter; yet it does not supersede it, but makes it rather a greater necessity. To this very end we are consecrated by the blood: that we may be purified inwardly by the Holy Ghost; and he who would make the completeness of the former act a substitute for the latter process, or a reason for neglecting it, has yet to learn what consecration means, what is the import of the blood which consecrates, and for what end we were chosen in Christ and called by His grace (Eph 1:4).

The thing which man calls sin may be easily obliterated or toned down into goodness. It deserved no expulsion from Paradise, no deluge, no Sodom-fire; it is a thing which the flames of Sinai greatly exaggerate, and of which Israel's history presents an exceptional picture. It is one of the mishaps of humanity, the enormity of which has been quite misreckoned by theologians, and the history of which, in Scripture, must be read with abatements and due allowances for oriental colouring! It is not a thing for the judge, but for the physician; not a thing for condemnation, but for pity. It deserves no hell, no divine wrath, no legal sentence; it needs no atonement, no blood, no cross, no substitution of life for life; mere incarnation as the expression of divine love to the unfortunate, and the intimation to the universe of God's all-comprehending fatherhood, and of Adamhood's union with God will be sufficient.

But that which God calls sin is something infinitely terrible, far beyond our ideas of misfortune and disease, something to which even Sodom and Sinai gave but faint expression. It is something which the law curses and the Judge condemns; something which needs a righteous pardon, a divine Saviour, and an almighty Spirit; something which can destroy a soul and ruin a world, which can, from one single drop, overflow earth for six thousand years, and fill hell eternally. It is that of whose hatefulness the blood and smoke and fire of the altar speak, which is "exceeding sinful," whose wages is death, the first and second death, and of whose balefulness the everlasting darkness is the witness.

He who would know holiness must understand sin; and he who would see sin as God sees it, and think of it as God does, must look at the cross and grave of the Son of God, and must know the meaning of Gethsemane and Golgotha.

Am I bound to think of sin as God thinks? Most certainly.

Have I no liberty of thinking otherwise? None. You may do so, if you choose to venture, but the consequences are fearful, for error is sin. We are not bound to think as man thinks. In this respect we have entire liberty; not tradition, but free thought may be our formula here. But we are bound to think as God thinks, not in one thing but in everything. Woe be to him that presumes to differ from God, or reckons it a light matter to be of one mind with Him, or tries to prove that the Bible is inaccurate or unintelligible, or but half-inspired, in order to release himself from the responsibility of receiving the whole truth of God and to afford him license to believe or disbelieve at pleasure, freed from the trammels of a fixed revelation.

The tendency of the present day is to underestimate sin and to misunderstand its nature. From the cross of Christ men strike out the very elements which imply the divine opinion of its evil. Sin is admitted to be an evil, greater or less according to circumstances; a hereditary poison, which time and earnestness will work out of the constitution; an unruly but inevitable appetite, which is to be corrected gradually by moral discipline and wholesome intellectual diet, rendered medicinal by a moderate infusion of the "religious element"; a sickening pain, sometimes in the conscience, sometimes in the heart, that is to be soothed by the dreamy mysticism, which, acting like spiritual chloroform, dulls the uneasiness without touching its seat; this is all!

Why a loving God should, for so slight and curable an evil, have given over our world for six thousand years to such sorrow, pain, tears, weariness, disease and death, as have overflowed it with so terrible a deluge, is a question which such a theory of evil leaves unanswered. Yet such are the representations of sin with which we find a large amount of the literature and the religion of our day penetrated. Humanity is struggling upward, nobly self-reliant! The race is elevating itself (for the Darwinian theory has found its way into religion), and Christianity is a useful help in this process of self-regeneration! Thus does many a prophet speak peace where there is none, bent on "healing the hurt" by the denial of its deadliness. Of what avail this calling evil good and good evil, this putting darkness for light and light for darkness, this putting bitter for sweet and sweet for bitter, will be in the great day of reckoning, a coming hour will show.

"Awake to righteousness, and sin not," is God's message to us (1 Cor 15:34). "Be ye holy; for I am holy" (1 Pt 1:16). "Present your bodies a living sacrifice, holy, acceptable unto God" (Rom 12:1). "Purge out . . . the old leaven, that ye may be a new lump" (1 Cor 5:7). "Let everyone that nameth the name of Christ depart from iniquity" (2 Tm 2:19). "Denying ungodliness and worldly lusts, . . . live soberly, righteously, and godly, in this present world" (Ti 2:12). "Be diligent that ye may be found in Him in peace, without spot and blameless" (2 Pt 3:14). "Let your conversation be as it becometh the gospel of Christ" (Phil 1:27). "Have no fellowship with the unfruitful works of darkness, but rather reprove them" (Eph 5:11). "Put ye on the Lord Jesus Christ, and make not provision for the flesh to fulfil the lusts thereof" (Rom 13:14). "I beseech you as strangers and pilgrims, abstain from fleshly lusts, which war against the soul" (1 Pt 2:11).

From sin, then, in every sense and aspect, God is calling us. As exceeding sinful, the abominable thing which He hates and will avenge, He warns us against it. He speaks to us as "shapen in iniquity and conceived in sin," carrying evil about with us, indeed, filled with it and steeped in it; not merely as diseased and requiring medicine, or unfortunate and requiring pity, but as guilty, under law, under sentence, dead in trespasses and sins, with inevitable judgment before us. He neither palliates nor aggravates our case, but calmly tells us the worst; showing us what we are, before calling us to be what He has purposed to make us. From all unholiness, from all uncleanness, from all unrighteousness, from all corruption, from all crooked ways, from all disobedience, from all filthiness of the flesh and spirit, He is calling us, in Christ Jesus His Son.

2

Christ for Us, the Spirit in Us

We noticed, in our last chapter, the difference between the divine and the human sides of Bible truth; we would, in this, turn to another distinction of no less importance: that between Christ's work for us and the Holy Spirit's work in us; between the legal or substitutionary and the moral or curative.

This is not the distinction between a divine element and a human one, but between two elements which are both equally divine, yet each of them, in its own way, bearing very directly on the sinner.

The two things are sometimes put in another form: Christ for us, and Christ in us. The meaning, however, is the same in both cases, for Christ in us (Col 1:27) is also the Holy Spirit in us, Christ having the Spirit without measure for Himself (Jn 3:34), and for us according to our need. An indwelling Christ and an indwelling Spirit are, though not the same thing, yet equivalent things. He who has the Son has the Spirit, indeed, and the Father also (Jn 14:23).

Christ for us is our one resting place. Not works, nor feelings, nor love, even though these may be the creation of the Spirit in us; not these in any sense; no, nor yet faith, whether as an act of our mind, or as the production of the Spirit, or as a substitute for righteousness—none of these can be our resting place.

This great truth is well brought out in a correspondence among Luther, Melancthon, and Brentius in the year 1531, which we translate and abridge. Brentius had been much perplexed on the subject of faith. It puzzled him. Christ justifies; faith justifies; how is this? Is faith a merit? Is it a work? Has it some justifying virtue in itself? Does it justify because it is the gift of God and the work of the Holy Spirit? Perplexed with these questions, he wrote to Melancthon and Luther. The replies of both are extant, neither of them long, Luther's very short. They go straight to the point, and deserve to be quoted as clear statements of the truth, and as specimens of the way in which these men of might dealt with the burdened spirits of their time. "I see," writes Melancthon,

> what is troubling you about faith. You stick to the fancy of Augustine, who, though right in rejecting the righteousness of human reason, imagines that we are justified by that fulfilling of the law which the Holy Spirit works in us. So you imagine that men are justified by faith, because it is by faith that we receive the Spirit, that thereafter we may be able to be just by that fulfillment of the law which the Spirit works. This imagination places justification in our fulfillment of the law, in our purity or perfection, although this renewal ought to follow faith. But do you turn your eyes from that renewal, and from the law altogether, to the promise and to Christ, and think that it is on Christ's account that we become just, that is, accepted before God, and that it is thus

we obtain peace of conscience, and not on account of that renewal? For even this renewing is insufficient (for justification). We are justified by faith alone, not because it is a root, as you write, but because it apprehends Christ, on account of whom we are accepted. This renewing, although it necessarily follows, yet does not pacify the conscience. Therefore not even love, though it is the fulfilling of the law, justifies, but only faith, not because it is some excellence in us, but only because it takes hold of Christ. We are justified, not on account of love, not on account of the fulfilling of the law, not on account of our renewal, although these are the gifts of the Holy Spirit, but on account of Christ; and Him we take hold of by faith alone.

Believe me, my Brentius, this controversy regarding the righteousness which is by faith is a mighty one, and little understood. You can only rightly comprehend it by turning your eyes entirely away from the law, and from Augustine's idea about our fulfilling the law, and by fixing them wholly upon the free promise, so as to see that it is on account of that promise and for Christ's sake that we are justified, that is, accepted, and obtain peace. This is the true doctrine, and that which glorifies Christ and wonderfully lifts up the conscience. I endeavoured to explain this in my *Apology*, but on account of the misrepresentations of adversaries, could not speak out so freely as I do now with you, though saying the very same thing. When could the conscience have peace and assured hope, if we are not justified till our renewal is perfected? What is this but to be justified by the law, and not by the free promise? In that discussion I said that to ascribe our justification to love is to ascribe it to our own work, understanding by that a work done in us by the Holy Ghost. For faith justifies, not because it is a new work of the Spirit in us, but because it apprehends Christ, on account of whom we are accepted, and not on account of the gifts of the Holy Spirit in us. Turn away from Augustine's idea, and you will easily see the reason for this; and I hope our *Apology* will somewhat help you, though I speak cautiously respecting matters so great, which are only to be to understood in the conflict of the conscience. By all means preach law and repentance to the people, but let not this true doctrine of the gospel be overlooked.

In the same strain writes Luther:

I am accustomed, my Brentius, for the better understanding of this point, to conceive this idea, that there is no quality in my heart at all, call it either faith or charity; but instead of these I set Christ Himself, and I say this is my righteousness. He is my quality and my formal righteousness, as they call it, so as to free myself from looking unto law or works, indeed, from looking at Christ Himself as a teacher or a giver. But I look at Him as gift and as doctrine to me, in Himself, so that in Him I have all things. He says, 'I am the way, and the truth, and the life.' He says not, 'I give thee the way, and the truth, and the life,' as if He were working on me from without. All these things He must be in me, abiding, living, and speaking in me, not through me or to me, that we may be 'the righteousness of God in Him' (2 Cor 5:21)—not in love, nor in the gifts and graces which follow.

To these letters Brentius replies, unfolding his conflicts to his beloved Philip:

Is not faith itself a work? . . . Does not the Lord say, "This is the work of God that ye believe'? . . . Justification then cannot be either by works or by faith. . . . Is it so? . . . Therefore justification must be on account of Christ alone, and not the excellence of our works. . . . But how can all this be? . . .

From childhood I had not been able to clear my thoughts on these points. Your letter and that of Luther showed me the truth. . . . Justification comes to us neither on account of our love nor our faith, but solely on account of Christ; and yet it comes through (by means of) faith. Faith does not justify as a work of goodness, but simply as a receiver of promised mercy. . . . We do not merit; we only obtain justification. . . . Faith is but the organ, the instrument, the medium; Christ alone is the satisfaction and the merit. Works are not satisfaction, nor merit, nor instrument; they are the utterance of a justification already received by faith."

Thus does the disciple expound the master's letter, and then adds some thoughts of his own. He fears lest, as popery perverted love, so the Reformation might come to pervert faith, putting it in the room of Christ, as a work or merit or quality, something in itself. Having finished the letter to his "most beloved Philip," and signed it, "thy Brentius," he starts another thought and adds a postscript which is well worth translating:

Just as I was finishing my letter, I remembered an argument of yours about works, to the effect that if we are justified by love, we can never have assurance because we can never love as we ought. In like manner I argue regarding faith as a work; if justification come to us through faith as a work, or merit, or excellence, we can never be assured about it, because we can never believe as we ought.

We have given some space to these extracts because the importance of the truth which they contain can hardly be overrated. They not only exhibit the distinction between Christ's work and the Spirit's work, but they do so with special reference to that point at which they are so often made to run into each other, to the darkening of many minds and the confusion of all Reformation theology. For how often did Luther reiterate that statement: "Faith justifies us, no, not even as a gift of the Holy Ghost, but solely on account of its reference to Christ. . . . Faith does not justify for its own sake, or because of any inherent virtue belonging to it." So long as this confusion exists, so long as men do not distinguish between Christ's work and the Spirit's work, so long as they lay any stress upon the quality or quantity of their act of faith, there can be not only no peace of conscience, but no progress in holiness, no bringing forth of good works. Of this confusion Arminianism, in its subtlest form, is the necessary offspring. For so long as men think to be justified by faith as a work, or as an act of their mind, or as a gift of the Spirit, they are seeking justification by something inherent, not by something imputed. To deny that it is inherent, because infused into them by the Spirit, is simply to cheat themselves with a play upon words, and to cheat themselves all the more effectually, because professing to honour the Spirit by ascribing to Him the infused quality or act, out of which they seek to extract their justification. In seeking justification or peace of conscience from something wrought in them by the Spirit, they are seeking these from that which is confessedly imperfect, and which God never gave for such a purpose; nay, they are rejecting the perfect righteousness of the Substitute, and so preventing the possibility of their doing any acceptable works at all. For if "the righteousness of the law can only be fulfilled in us," as the fruit of our acceptance of the imputed righteousness of the Son of God, then there can be no righteous thing done by us till we have realised the position of men to whom the great truth of "Christ for us," "Jehovah our righteousness," has become the basis of all reconciliation with God. This form of error is the more subtle because its victims are not walking in sin, but doing all manner of outward service, and exhibiting outward goodness in many forms, regarding which we shall only say that they are not pleasant to God, and as "they are not done as God hath willed and commanded them to be done, we doubt not but they have the nature of sin."[1]

Some of the soundest Christian divines have left on record their complaint as to the mistakes in this matter of faith prevailing in their day, and as to the charge of Antinomianism brought against those who, in stating justification, refuse to qualify the apostolic formula, "to him that worketh not, but believeth." Traill thus wrote, now nearly two centuries ago, "If we say that faith in Jesus Christ is neither work, nor condition, nor qualification in justification, and that in its very act it is a renouncing of all things but the gift of grace, the fire is kindled; so that it is come to this, that he that will not be Antichristian must be called an Antinomian."

How strongly does this same divine state the truth in another place. When addressing a perplexed inquirer he says, "If he say that he cannot believe on Jesus Christ . . . you tell him that believing on Jesus Christ is no work, but a resting on Jesus Christ." How sharply does he rebuke those who would mix up the imputed and the infused: "They seem to be jealous lest God's grace and Christ's righteousness have too much room, and men's works too little in the business of justification." See the whole of Traill's letter on "Justification vindicated from the charge of Antinomianism." An old anonymous writer, a little later than Traill, uses this expression: "The Scriptures consider faith not as a work of ours, but set in opposition to every work, whether of body or mind: 'To him that worketh not, but believeth.'"

That we believe through grace that faith is the gift of God does not prove faith to be a work of ours, any more than Christ's raising of Lazarus proved resurrection to be a work of the dead man. The divine infusion of life in the one case, and the divine impartation of faith in the other, so far from showing that there must be a work in either, indicates very plainly that there could

---

1. Article 13 of the Church of England.

not be any such thing. The work comes after the believing, and as the fruit of it. "Faith worketh by love"; that is, the believing soul shows its faith by works of love.

Yes, faith works; so also does love, so also does hope. These all work, and we read of "the work of faith," that is, work to which faith prompts us; the "labour of love," that is, the toil to which love impels us; the "patience of hope," that is, the patience which hope enables us to exercise. But is faith a work because it works? Is love a toil because it toils? Is hope patience because it makes us patient? Israel's looking to the brazen serpent was a ceasing from all remedies, and letting health pour itself into the body by the eye. Was the opening of the eye a work? The gospel does not command us to do anything in order to obtain life, but bids us live by that which another has done; and the knowledge of its life-giving truth is not labour but rest—rest of soul—rest which is the root of all true labour; for in receiving Christ we do not work in order to rest, but we rest in order to work. In believing, we cease to work for pardon, in order that we may work from it; and what incentive to work, as well as joy in working, can be greater than an ascertained and realised forgiveness?

That there are works done before faith we know, but regarding them we know that they profit nothing, "for without faith it is impossible to please God." That there are works done after faith we also know, and they are well pleasing to God, for they are the works of believing men. But, as to any work intermediate between these two, Scripture is silent; and against transforming faith into a work the whole theology of the Reformation protested, as either a worthless verbal quibble, or as the subtlest dregs of popery.

Truly faith comes from God. The revelation which we believe, and the power of believing that revelation, are both divine. The Holy Spirit has written the Scriptures, and sent them to us to be believed for salvation; faith cometh by hearing, and hearing by the Word of God. He quickens the dead soul that it may believe; and then after its believing He comes in and dwells. Hence, we are said to receive the Spirit by "the hearing of faith" (Gal 3:2). He opens our hand to receive the gift, and He places the gift in our hand when thus opened by Himself. Never let us forget that while faith is the result of the Spirit's work in us, it is as truly the receiver of Him as the indwelling Spirit, and that in proportion to our faith will be the measure of the Spirit we shall possess. This is another of the many twofold truths or processes of Scripture: the Spirit works to enable us to believe, and we in believing receive Him and all His gifts, in greater or less abundance, according to our faith.

This twofold, sometimes threefold, aspect of a truth ought not to perplex us; still less ought it to lead us to magnify one of these at the expense of the others, or to attempt a reconciliation of the three by a denial of one, and an explaining away of texts that stand in our way. Let us admit the whole, and accept the passages as they stand. Sometimes, for example, our renewal is connected with the Spirit (Ti 3:5), sometimes with Christ's resurrection (1 Pt 1:3), sometimes with the word of truth (Eph 1:13), and sometimes with faith (Jn 1:12). Sometimes it is spoken of as God's work (Ps 51:10), sometimes as our own (Ezek 18:31; Eph 4:24), sometimes as the work of ministers (Phil 10), sometimes as the effect of the gospel (1 Cor 4:15). So it is with conversion, with salvation, and with sanctification. These are all spoken of in connection with God, with Christ, with the Spirit, with the Word, with faith, with hope; and each of these aspects must be studied, not evaded.

John Calvin does not hesitate to speak of regeneration and repentance being the result of faith.[2] And Latimer writes, "We be born again. How? Not by a mortal seed, but by an immortal. What is this immortal seed? The Word of the living God. Thus cometh our new birth." In stating one side of the truth,

---

2. *Institutes* 3.3.1. See the whole third book.

these divines did not set aside the other. They taught renovation, through the truth and through faith, and they also taught renovation by the power of the Holy Ghost. They taught man's need of the Spirit in order to faith, and they also proclaimed the gift of the Spirit as the result of faith.

But manifold as are these aspects, they all bear upon us personally, directly or indirectly affecting and carrying out our quickening, our healing, our joy, our comfort, and our holiness. There is no speculation in any of them, and it is truth, not opinion, that they present to us. Whatever amount of unreal religion may be in us, it is not because of any defect in the Word, any cloudiness in the gospel, any scantiness or straitness in the divine liberality, and lack in the fullness of Him in whom it hath pleased the Father that all fullness should dwell. He has made provision for our being made like Himself, and therefore He calls us to this likeness. The standard is high, but it does not admit of being lowered. The model is divine, but so is the strength given for conformity to it. Our responsibility to be holy is great, but not greater than the means provided for its full attainment.

In Christ dwells all the fullness of Godhead bodily. He has the Holy Spirit for us, and this Spirit He gives freely and plenteously; for that which we receive is "grace according to the measure of the gift of Christ." The early saints were "filled with joy, and with the Holy Ghost" (Acts 13:52), and we are to be "filled with the Spirit" (Eph 5:18), for it is the Holy Ghost Himself, not certain influences that are given unto us (Rom 5:5). He falls on us (Acts 8:16; 11:15); He is shed forth on us (Acts 2:33); He is poured out on us (Ezek 39:29; Acts 10:45); we are baptized with the Holy Ghost (Acts 11:16). He is the earnest of our inheritance (Eph 1:14); He seals us (Eph 1:13), imprinting on us the divine image and superscription; He teaches (1 Cor 2:13); He reveals (1 Cor 2:10); He reproves (Jn 16:8); He strengthens (Eph 3:16); He makes us fruitful (Gal 5:22); He searches (1 Cor 2:10); He strives (Gn 6:3); He sanctifies (1 Cor 6:11); He leads (Rom 8:14;

Ps 143:3); He instructs (Neh 9:20); He speaks (1 Tm 4:1; Rv 2:7); He demonstrates (or proves) (1 Cor 2:4); He intercedes (Rom 8:26); He quickens (Rom 8:11); He gives utterance (Acts 2:4); He creates (Ps 104:30); He comforts (Jn 14:26); He sheds abroad the love of God in our hearts (Rom 5:5); He renews (Ti 3:5). He is the Spirit of holiness (Rom 1:4), the Spirit of wisdom and understanding (Is 11:2; Eph 1:17), the Spirit of truth (Jn 14:17), the Spirit of knowledge (Is 11:2), the Spirit of grace (Heb 10:29), the Spirit of glory (1 Pt 4:14), the Spirit of our God (1 Cor 6:11), the Spirit of the living God (2 Cor 3:3), the good Spirit (Neh 9:20), the Spirit of Christ (1 Pt 1:11), the Spirit of adoption (Rom 8:15), the Spirit of life (Rv 11:11), and the Spirit of His Son (Gal 4:6).

Such is the Holy Spirit by whom we are sanctified (2 Th 2:13), "the eternal Spirit" by whom "Christ offered Himself without spot to God" (Heb 9:14). Such is the Holy Spirit by whom we are "sealed unto the day of redemption" (Eph 4:30), the Spirit who makes us His habitation (Eph 2:22), who dwells in us (2 Tm 1:14), by whom we are kept looking to and looking for Christ and by whom we are made to "abound in hope" (Rom 15:13).

On the right receiving and entertaining of this heavenly Guest, much of a holy life depends. Let us bid Him welcome—not vexing, nor resisting, nor grieving, nor quenching Him, but loving Him and delighting in His love ("the love of the Spirit," Rom 15:30), so that our life may be a living in the Spirit (Gal 5:25), a walking in the Spirit (Gal 5:16), a praying in the Spirit (Jude 20). While distinguishing Christ's work for us and the Spirit's work in us, and so preserving our conscious pardon unbroken, yet let us not separate the two by any interval; but allowing both to do their work, let us "follow peace with all men, and holiness, without which no man shall see the Lord" (Heb 12:14), keeping our hearts in "the fellowship of the Spirit" (Phil 2:1), and delighting ourselves in "the communion of the Holy Ghost" (2 Cor 13:14).

The double form of expression, bringing out the mutual or

reciprocal indwelling of Christ and of the Spirit in us, is worthy of special note. Christ in us (Col 1:27) is the one side; we in Christ is the other (2 Cor 5:17; Gal 2:20). The Holy Spirit in us (Rom 8:9) is the one aspect; we live in the Spirit (Gal 5:25) is the other. Nay, further, this twofold expression is used of Godhead also, in these remarkable words: "Whosoever shall confess that Jesus is the Son of God, God dwelleth in him, and he in God" (1 Jn 4:15).

It would seem as if no figure, however strong and full, could adequately express the closeness of contact, the nearness of relationship, the entire oneness into which we are brought, in receiving the divine testimony to the person and work of the Son of God. Are we not then most strongly committed to a life of holiness, as well as furnished with all the supplies needful for carrying it out? With such a fullness of strength and life at our disposal, what a responsibility is ours! "What manner of persons ought we to be in all holy conversation and godliness!" And if to all this we add the prospects presented to us, the hope of the advent and the kingdom and the glory, we shall feel ourselves compassed on every side with the motives, materials, and appliances best fitted for making us what we are meant to be, "a royal priesthood, an holy nation, a peculiar people" (1 Pt 2:9),[3] "zealous of good works" here (Ti 2:14), and possessors of "glory and honor, and immortality" hereafter (Rom 2:7).

---

3. It is remarkable that these words were first used regarding Israel (Ex 19:5, 6; Dt 7:6), showing us that Old Testament saints did not stand on a lower level than New Testament ones. Most of the expressions used concerning the church's privileges are Old Testament ones, borrowed from Israel's privileges. To the latter belonged the heavenly kingdom (Mt 5:3; 8:11), the sonship (Ex 4:22, 23), the adoption, the glory, and the promises (Rom 9:4).

3

The Root and Soil of Holiness

Every plant must have both soil and root. Without both of these, there can be no life, no growth, no fruit.

Holiness must have these. The root is "peace with God"; the soil in which that root strikes itself, and out of which it draws the vital sap, is the free love of God, in Christ Jesus our Lord. "Rooted in love" is the apostle's description of a holy man. Holiness is not austerity or gloom; these are as alien to it as levity and flippancy. Nor is it the offspring of terror, or suspense, or uncertainty, but peace, conscious peace, and this peace must be rooted in grace; it must be the consequence of our having ascertained, upon sure evidence, the forgiving love of God. He who would lead us into holiness must "guide our feet into the way of peace" (Lk 1:79). He must show us how we, "being delivered out of the hand of our enemies," may serve God "without fear, in holiness and righteousness before Him, all the days of our life" (Lk 1:74, 75). He who would do this must also "give us the knowledge of salvation, by the remission of sins." He must tell us how, through "the tender mercy of our God . . . the dayspring from on high hath visited us, to give light to them that sit in darkness and in the shadow of death" (Lk 1:78, 79).

In carrying out the great work of making us holy, God speaks to us, as "the God of peace" (Rom 16:20), "the very God of peace" (1 Th 5:23), and as being Himself "our peace" (Eph 2:14). That which we receive from Him, as such, is not merely "peace with God" (Rom 5:1), but "the peace of God" (Phil 4:7), the thing which the Lord calls "My peace," "My joy" (Jn 14:27; 15:11). It is in connection with the exhortation, "Be perfect," that the apostle sets down the gracious assurance: "The God of love and peace shall be with you" (2 Cor 13:11). "These things I will that thou affirm constantly," says the apostle, speaking of "the grace of God that bringeth salvation," "the kindness and love of God our Saviour," the "mercy of God," "justification by His grace," in order that (such is the force of the Greek) "they which have believed in God might be careful to maintain good works" (Ti 3:8).

In this "peace with God" there is, of course, contained salvation, forgiveness, deliverance from the wrath to come. But these, though precious, are not terminating points; not ends, but beginnings; not the top but the bottom of that ladder which rests its foot upon the new sepulchre wherein never man was laid, and its top against the gate of the holy city. He, therefore, who is contenting himself with these, has not yet learned the true purport of the gospel, nor the end which God, from eternity, had in view when preparing for us such a redemption as that which He has accomplished for the sons of men, through His only begotten Son, "who gave Himself for us, that He might redeem us from all iniquity."

Without these, holiness is impossible, so that we may say this at least, that it is through them that holiness is made practicable, for the legal condition of the sinner, as under wrath, stood as a barrier between him and the possibility of holiness. So long as he was under condemnation, the law prohibited the approach of everything that would make him holy. The law bars salvation, except on the fulfillment of its claims; so it bars holiness, until the great satisfaction to its claims has been recognised by the individual, that is, until he has believed the divine testimony to the atonement of the cross, and so been personally set free from condemnation. The law pronounces against the idea of holiness in an unforgiven man. It protests against it as an incongruity, and as an injury to righteousness. If, then, a pardoned man's remaining unholy seem strange, much more so a holy man's remaining unpardoned. The sinner's legal position must be set right before his moral position can be touched. Condition is one thing; character is another. The sinner's standing before God, either in favour or disfavour, either under grace or under wrath, must first be dealt with before his inner renewal can be carried on. The judicial must precede the moral.

Hence, it is of pardon that the gospel first speaks to us, for the question of pardon must first be settled before we proceed to others. The adjustment of the relationship between us and God is an indispensable preliminary, both on God's part and on ours. There must be friendship between us before He can bestow or we receive His indwelling Spirit; for on the one hand, the Spirit cannot make His dwelling in the unforgiven; and on the other, the unforgiven must be so occupied with the one question of forgiveness, that they are not at leisure to attend to anything till this has been finally settled in their favour. The man who knows that the wrath of God is still upon him—or, which is the same thing practically, is not sure whether it has been turned away or not—is really not in a condition to consider other questions, however important, if he has any true idea of the magnitude and terribleness of the anger of Him who is a consuming fire.

The divine order, then, is first pardon, then holiness; first peace with God, and then conformity to the image of that God with whom we have been brought to be at peace. For as likeness to God is produced by beholding His glory (2 Cor 3:18), and as we cannot look upon Him till we know that He has ceased to condemn us, and as we cannot trust Him till we know that He is gracious; so we cannot be transformed into His image till we have received pardon at His hands. Reconciliation is indispensable to resemblance; personal friendship must begin a holy life.

If such be the case, pardon cannot come too soon, even were the guilt of an unpardoned state not reason enough for any amount of urgency in obtaining it without delay. Nor can we too strongly insist upon the divine order above referred to: first peace, then holiness—peace as the foundation of holiness, even in the case of the chief of sinners.

Some do not object to a reputable man obtaining immediate peace, but they object to a profligate getting it at once! So it has always been; the old taunt is still on the lip of the modern Pharisee: "He is gone to be a guest with a man that is a sinner," and the Simons of our day speak within themselves and say, "This man, if He were a prophet, would have known who and what manner of woman this is that toucheth Him, for she is a sinner" (Lk 7:39). But what then of Manasseh, and Magdalene, and Saul, and the woman of Sychar, and the jailor, and the men of Jerusalem, whose hands were red with blood? Were they not trusted with a free and immediate peace? Did not the very essence and strength of the gospel's curative and purifying power lie in the freeness, the promptness, the certainty of the peace which it brought to these "chief of sinners"? "So you say you have found Christ, and have peace with God?" said one who claimed the name of "evangelical," to a poor profligate who, only a few weeks before, had been drawn to the cross. "I have indeed," said the poor man. "I have found Him, I have peace, and I know it." "Know it!" said the divine, "and have you the presumption to tell me this? I have been a respectable member of a church for thirty years, and have not got peace nor assurance yet, and you, who have been a profligate most of your life, say that you have peace with God!" "Yes, I have been as bad as a man can well be, but I have believed the gospel, and that gospel is good news for the like of me; and if I have no right to peace, I had better go back to my sins, for if I cannot get peace as I am, I shall never get it at all." "It's all a delusion," said the other. "Do you think that God would give a sinner like you peace, and not give it to me who have been doing all I can to get it for so many years?" "You are such a respectable man," said the other, in unconscious irony, "that you can get on without peace and pardon, but a wretch like me cannot. If my peace is a delusion, it cannot be a bad one, for it makes me leave off sin, and makes me pray and read my Bible. Since I got it, I have turned over a new leaf." "It won't last," said the other. "Well, but it is a good thing while it does last, and it is strange to see the like of you trying to take from me the only thing that ever did me good. It looks as if you would be glad to see me going back to my old sins. You never tried to bring me to Christ, and, now when I have come to Him, you are doing all you can to take me away. But I'll stick to Him in spite of you."

Some speak as if it were imperiling morality to let the sinner obtain immediate peace with God. If the peace be false, morality may be compromised by men pretending to the possession of a peace which is yet no peace. But, in that case, the evil complained of is the result of the hollowness, not the suddenness, of the peace, and can afford no ground for objecting to speedy peace, unless speedy peace is of necessity false, and unless the mere length of the process is security for the genuineness of the result. The existence of false peace is no argument against the true, and what we affirm is, that true peace can neither be too speedy nor too sure.

Others speak as if no sinner could be trusted with pardon till he has undergone a certain amount of preliminary mental suffering, more or less in duration and in intensity according to circumstances. It would be dangerous to the interests of morality to let him obtain an immediate pardon and, especially, to be sure of it, or to rejoice in it. If the man has been previously moral in life, they would not object to this; but they question the profligate's right to present peace, and protest against the propriety of it on grounds of subtle morality. They argue for delay, to give him time to improve before he ventures to speak of pardon. They insist upon a long season of preparatory conflict, years of sad suspense and uncertainty, in order to qualify the prodigal for his father's embrace, and to prevent the unseemly spectacle of a sinner this week rejoicing in the forgiveness of his sins, who last week was wallowing in the mire. This season of delay, during which they would prohibit the sinner from assuring himself of God's free love, they consider the proper safeguard of a free gospel, and the needful guarantee for the sinner's future humility and holiness.

Is not, then, the position taken up by these men substantially that adopted by the scribes, when they murmured at the Lord's gracious familiarity with the unworthy, saying, "This man receiveth sinners, and eateth with them"? And is it not in great measure coincident with the opinion of popish theologians respecting the danger to morality from the doctrine of immediate justification through simple faith in the justifying work of Christ?

When Bishop Gardiner, the popish persecutor, lay dying in 1555, Day, Bishop of Chichester, "began to comfort him," says Foxe, "with words of God's promise, and free justification by the blood of Christ." "What," said the dying Romanist, "will *you* open that gap?" meaning that inlet of evil. "To me and others in my case you may speak of it, but once open this window to the people, then farewell all good."

The apostles evidently had great confidence in the gospel. They gave it fair play, and spoke it out in all its absolute freeness, as men who could trust it for its moral influence, as well as for its saving power, and who felt that the more speedily and certainly its good news were realised by the sinner, the more would that moral influence come into play. They did not hide it, nor trammel it, nor fence it round with conditions, as if doubtful of the policy of preaching it freely. "Be it known unto you," they said, "men and brethren, that through this Man is preached unto you the forgiveness of sins, and by Him all that believe are justified" (Acts 13:38, 39). They had no misgivings as to its bearings on morality, nor were they afraid of men believing it too soon, or getting too immediate relief from it. The idea does not seem to have entered their mind, that men could betake themselves to Christ too soon, or too confidently, or without sufficient preparation. Their object in preaching it was, not to induce men to commence a course of preparation for receiving Christ, but to receive Him at once and on the spot; not to lead them through the long avenue of a gradually amended life to the cross of the Sin-bearer, but to bring them at once into contact with the cross, that sin in them might be slain, the old man crucified, and a life of true morality begun. As the strongest motive to a holy life, they preached the cross. They knew that, "The cross once seen is death to every vice," and in the interests of holiness, they stood and pleaded with men to take the proffered peace.

It is no disparagement to morality to say that good works are not the way to Christ. It is no slighting of the sacraments to say that they are not the sinner's resting-place, so neither is it any deprecation of devotion, or repentance, or prayer, to say that they are not qualifying processes which fit the sinner for approaching the Saviour, either as making the sinner more acceptable or Christ more willing to receive. Still less is it derogating from the usefulness or the blessedness of these exercises, in their proper place and office, to say that they are often the refuges of self-righteousness, pretexts which the sinner makes use of to excuse his guilt in not at once taking salvation from the hands of Jesus. We do not undervalue love because we say a man is not justified by love, but by faith. We do not discourage prayer, because we preach that a man is not justified by prayer, but by faith. When we say that believing is not working, but a ceasing from work, we do not mean that the believing man is not to work, but that he is not to work for pardon, but to take it freely, and that he is to believe before he works, for works done before believing are not pleasing to God.

Is it the case that the sinner cannot be trusted with the gospel? In one sense this is true. He cannot be trusted with anything. He abuses everything. He turns everything to bad account. He makes everything the minister of sin. But if he cannot be trusted with the gospel, can he be trusted with the law? If he cannot be trusted with grace, can he be trusted with righteousness? He cannot be trusted with an immediate pardon; can he be trusted with a tardy one? He cannot be trusted with faith; can he be trusted with doubt? He cannot be trusted with peace; can he be trusted with gloom and trouble? He cannot be trusted with assurance; can he be trusted with suspense, and will uncertainty do for him what certainty cannot?

That which he can, after all, best be trusted with, is the gospel. He has abused it, he may abuse it, but he is less likely to abuse it than anything else. It appeals to deeper, stronger, and more numerous motives than all other things together.[1]

Hence, the apostles trusted the gospel with the sinner, and

---

1. The teaching of some in the present day seems fitted, that of others intended, to hinder assurance. Assurance, say some, is impossible. Not impossible, say others, but very hard of attainment; not only very hard, but very long of being reached, requiring at least some thirty or forty years of prayer and good works. Very dangerous, say others, introducing presumption, and sure to end in apostasy. I confess I do not see how my being thoroughly persuaded that a holy God loves me with a holy love, and has forgiven me all my sins, has a tendency to evil (even though I may have reached that conclusion quickly). It seems, of all truths, one of the likeliest to make me holy, to kindle love, to stimulate to good works, and to abase all pride; whereas uncertainty in this matter enfeebles me, darkens me, bewilders me, incapacitates me for service or, at the best, sets me striving to work my way into the favour of God, under the influence of a subordinate and mercenary class of motives, which can do

the sinner with the gospel, so unreservedly, and (as many in our day would say) unguardedly. "To him that worketh not, but believeth, his faith is counted for righteousness," was a bold statement. It is that of one who had great confidence in the gospel which he preached, who had no misgivings as to its unholy tendencies, if men would but give it fair play. He Himself always preached it as one who believed it to be the power of God unto holiness, no less than unto salvation.

That this is the understanding of the New Testament, the "mind of the Spirit," requires no proof. Few would in words deny it to be so; only they state the gospel so timorously, so warily, so guardedly, with so many conditions, terms, and reservations, that by the time they have finished their statement, they have left no good news in that which they set out with announcing as "the gospel of the grace of God."

The more fully that the gospel is preached, in the grand old apostolic way, the more likely is it to accomplish the results which it did in the apostolic days. The gospel is the proclamation of free love; the revelation of the boundless charity of God. Nothing less than this will suit our world; nothing else is so likely to touch the heart, to go down to the lowest depths of depraved humanity, as the assurance that the sinner has been loved—loved by God, loved with a righteous love, loved with a free love that makes no bargain as to merit, or fitness, or goodness. "Herein is love, not that we loved God, but that He loved us!" (1 Jn 4:10). As the lord of the vineyard, after sending servant upon servant to the husbandmen in vain, sent at last his "one son, his well-beloved" (Mk 12:6), so, law having failed, God has dispatched to us the message of His love, as that which is by far the likeliest to secure His ends. With nothing less than this free love will He trust our fallen race. He will not trust them with law, or judgment, or

---

nothing but keep me dreading and doubting all the days of my life, leaving me, perhaps, at the close, in hopeless darkness.

terror (though these are well in their place), but He will trust them with His love! Not with a stinted or conditional love, with half pardons, or an uncertain salvation, or a tardy peace, or a doubtful invitation, or an all but impracticable amnesty—not with these does He cheat the heavy laden; not with these will He mock the weary sons of men. He wants them to be holy, as well as safe, and He knows that there is nothing in heaven or earth so likely to produce holiness, under the teaching of the Spirit of holiness, as the knowledge of His own free love. It is not law, but "the love of Christ," that constraineth! "The strength of sin is the law" (1 Cor 15:56), so the strength of holiness is deliverance from the law (Rom 7:6). Yet are we not "without law" (1 Cor 9:21), neither yet "under the law" (Rom 6:14), but "under grace," that we should "serve in newness of Spirit, and not in the oldness of the letter."

Thus Calvin writes, "Consciences obey the law, not constrained by the necessity of law, but, being made free from the yoke of law, they voluntarily obey the will of God. They are in perpetual terror as long as they are under the dominion of the law, and are never disposed to obey God with delighted eagerness unless they have first received this liberty."[2] "Not to be under the law," says Luther, "is to do good and abstain from evil, not through the compulsion of law, but by free love and with gladness." "If any man ask me," says Tyndale, "seeing faith justifies me, why I work, I answer, love compelleth me; for as long as my soul feeleth what love God hath showed me in Christ, I cannot but love God again, and His will and commandments, and of love work them; nor can they seem hard to me."[3] "When faith hath bathed a man's heart in the blood of Christ, it is so mollified that it quickly dissolves into tears of godly sorrow; so that if Christ but turn and look upon him, oh, then with Peter he

---

2. *Institutes* 3.19.4.
3. Preface to Exodus.

goes out and weeps bitterly. And this is true gospel mourning; this is right evangelical repenting."[4]

But so many (it is said) of those who were awakened under the preaching of this very free gospel have gone back, that suspicions arise as to whether it may not be the ultra-freeness of the gospel preached that has produced the evil. It is suggested that, had the gospel been better guarded both before and behind, we should have seen fewer falls and less inconsistency. To this our answer is ready. Multitudes "went back" from our Lord, yet no one could blame His preaching. There were many grievous corruptions in the early church, yet we do not connect these with apostolic doctrine. Our Lord's parable of the sower implies that, however good the seed might be, and careful the sower, there would be stony-ground hearers and thorny-ground hearers going a certain length and then turning back, so that the backslidings complained of are such as the apostles experienced, such as our Lord led us to anticipate, under the preaching of His own full gospel.

Further than this, however, we add that, while the preaching of a guarded gospel may lead to no backslidings, it will accomplish no awakenings; so that the question will come to be this: is it not better to have some fallings away when many are aroused, than to have no falling away, because none have been shaken? The question as to what kind of teaching results in fewest backslidings is, no doubt, an important one; but still it is subordinate to the main one: what preaching produces, upon the whole, the most conversions, and brings most glory to God? Apostasies will occur in the best of churches, bringing with them scandal to the name of Jesus, and suspicion of the gospel as the cause of all the evil. But is this a new thing in the earth? Is it not one of the things that strikingly identify us with Corinth, and Sardis, and Laodicea? A minister who has never

---

[4]. Fisher's *Marrow of Modern Divinity*.

had his heart wounded with apostasy, who knows nothing of the disappointment of cherished hopes, has too good reason to suspect that there is something sadly wrong, and that the reason of there being no backslidings in his flock, is because death is reigning. Where all is silence or sleep, where the preaching does not shake and penetrate, there will be fewer fallings away; but the reason is, that there was nothing to fall away from. "Where are your converts now?" was the question put to a faithful minister who had had to mourn the fall of some who once "ran well." "Just where they were: the true still holding fast; the untrue showing themselves." It was meant as a taunt, but it was a taunt which might have been cast at apostles. It was a taunt which carried comfort with it, as reminding the faithful minister of apostolic disappointment, and so bringing him into fellowship with Paul himself, and as recalling the blessed fact that though some had fallen, more were standing.

The whole Galatian church had lapsed into error and sin. How does the apostle cure the evil? By fencing or paring down the gospel, and making it less free? No, but by reiterating its freeness; nay, stating it more freely than ever. How free does he represent it in the Epistle! Hence, Luther chose it for comment, as the one best suiting himself.

Some ask the question: "Is it not a suspicious sign of your gospel, that any of the hearers of it should say, 'May we continue in sin, that grace may abound'?" On the contrary, it is a safe sign of it. Had it not been very like Paul's gospel, it would not have led to the same inquiry with which the apostle's preaching was met. The restricted, guarded, conditional gospel, which some give us, as the ultimatum of their good news, would have suggested no such thought as that which the sixth chapter of Romans was written to obviate. The argument of the apostle, in such a case, becomes unmeaning and superfluous, and hence that statement which prompts some reviler to ask the question: "Shall we sin, because we are not under the law, but under grace?" (Rom 6:15) is not at all unlikely to be the authentic Pauline gospel, the genuine doctrine of apostolic antiquity.

4

Strength against Sin

Men live in sin, and yet they have the secret thought that it ought not to be so, that they ought to get rid of it. Even those that have not the law, in this respect "are a law unto themselves," for "the work of the law [that is, each thing the law enjoins us to do] is written in their hearts; their conscience also bearing witness, and their thoughts struggling with each other, either accusing or excusing" (Rom 2:15).

The groan of humanity, as well as the groan of creation, by reason of sin, has been deep and long. Not always loud; often an undertone, more often drowned in laughter, but still terribly real.

Sin as disease, infectious and hereditary, sin as guilt, inferring divine condemnation and doom, has been acknowledged; and along with the acknowledgement, the sad consciousness has existed that the race was not made for sin, and that man himself, not God, had wrought the wrong. Men in all ages, and of all religions, have in some poor way, put in their protest against sin, "knowing the judgment of God, that they which commit such things are worthy of death" (Rom 1:32). The fallen sons of Adam, though haters of God and of His law (Rom 1:30), have thus unconsciously become witnesses against themselves, and unwittingly taken the side of God and of His law.

All through the ages has this struggle gone on between the love and the dread of sin, the delight in lust, and the sense of degradation because of it; men clasping the poisoned robe, yet wishing to tear it off; their life steeped in the evil, yet their words so often lavished upon the good.

With much warmth did the ancient pagan wisdom of Greece and Rome utter itself against vice, with deep pathos at times describing the conflict with self, and the victory over the unruly will and the irregular appetite. But it suggested no remedy, and promised no power in aid. It could only say, "Fight on." Philosophy was helpless in its encounters with human evil, and in its sympathies with earthly sorrow. It looked on, and spoke many a true word, but it wrought no cure, it healed no wounds, it rooted out no sin. It was the exhibition of weakness, not of power, the mere cry of human helplessness.

Romish devotees, with fastings and flagellations, in addition to earnest words, have tried to extirpate the wrong and nourish the right. Groping after righteousness, yet not knowing what righteousness is, nor how it comes to us, they have built themselves up in self-righteousness. Professing to seek holiness, without understanding its nature, they have snared themselves in delusions which bring no purity. Bent, as they say, upon "mortifying the flesh," falsely identifying "the flesh" with the mere body, and working upon the theology which teaches that it is the body which ruins the soul, they lay great stress on weakening and macerating the corporeal frame, not knowing that they are thus feeding sin, fostering pride, making the body less fit to be the helpmeet of the soul, and thereby producing unholiness of the darkest type in the eye of God. By rules of no gentle kind: by terror, by pain, by visions of death and the grave, by pictures of a fiercely flaming hell, by the denial of all certainty in pardon, they have sought to terrify or force themselves into goodness. By long prayers, by bitter practices of self-denial, by slow chants at midnight or early morn in dim cathedrals, by frequent sacraments, by deep study of old fathers, by the cold of wintry solitude, by multiplied deeds of merit and will-worship, they have thought to expel the demon, and to eradicate "the ineradicable taint of sin."

But success has not come in this way. The enterprise was a high but fearful one and the men knew not how terrible it was. They had quite underrated the might of the enemy, while overestimating their own. The resources of the two sides were indeed unequal. Not Leonidas against the myriads of Persia, nor the old Roman three who held the bridge against the Etruscan host could be compared to this. It might seem but the feeble aberrations of one poor human heart that they were dealing with, but they knew not what these indicated—what the power of a human will is for evil; what is man's hostility to God; what is the vitality of sin; what is the exasperating tendency of naked law, and the elasticity of evil under legal compression; what is the tenacity of man's resistance to goodness and to the law of goodness; what all these together must be when fostered from beneath, and backed by the resources of hell.

In all this, there is not one thought of grace or divine free love, no recognition of forgiveness as the root of holiness. Man's philosophy and man's religion have never suggested this. It would seem as if man could not trust himself with this, and could not believe that God would trust him with it. He has no idea of barriers against sin, save in the shape of walls, chains, and bars of iron, of torture, threats, and wrath. On these alone he relies. He is slow to learn that all legal deterrents are in their very nature irritants, with no power to produce or enforce anything but a constrained externalism. The interposition of forgiving love, in absolute completeness and freeness, is resisted as an encouragement to evil-doing; and, at the most, only in a very conditional and restricted form is grace allowed to come into play. The dynamics of grace have never been reduced to a formula; they are supposed incapable of being so set down. That God should act in any other character than as the rewarder of the deserving and the punisher of the undeserving; that He should go down into the depths of a human heart, and there touch springs which were reckoned inaccessible or perilous to deal with; that His gospel should throw itself upon something nobler than man's fear of wrath, and begin by proclaiming pardon as the first step to holiness—this is so incredible to man, that, even with the Bible and the cross before his eyes, he turns away from it as foolishness. Nevertheless this is "the more excellent way,"—indeed, the true and only way of getting rid of sin. Forgiveness of sins, in believing God's testimony to the finished propitiation of the cross, is not simply indispensable to a holy life, in the way of removing terror and liberating the soul from the pressure of guilt, but of imparting an impulse, and a motive, and a power which nothing else could do. Forgiveness at the end or in the middle, a partial forgiveness, or an uncertain forgiveness, or a grudging forgiveness, would be of no avail; it would only tantalise and mock. But a complete forgiveness, presented in such a way as to carry its own certainty along with it to every one who will take it at the hands of God—this is a power in the earth, a power against self, a power against sin, a power over the flesh, a power for holiness, such as no amount of suspense or terror could create.

It is to this that our Lord refers, once and again, when dealing with the Pharisees, those representatives of a human standard of goodness as contrasted with a divine. How deep is the significance of such statements as these: "When they had nothing to pay, he frankly forgave them both" (Lk 7:42); "Her sins, which are many, are forgiven" (Lk 7:47); "The lord of that servant was moved with compassion, and loosed him, and forgave him the debt" (Mt 18:27); "Neither do I condemn thee, go and sin no more" (Jn 8:11); "I came not to call the righteous, but sinners to repentance" (Lk 5:32); "The Son of man is come to seek and to save that which was lost" (Lk 19:10); "God so loved the world, that He gave His only begotten Son" (Jn 3:16); "I came not to judge the world, but to save the world" (Jn 12:47). It is to this also that the apostles so often refer in their discourses and Epistles: "Who His own self bare our sins in His own body on the tree, that we, being dead to sins, should live unto righteousness" (1 Pt 2:24); "Through this man is preached unto you the forgiveness of sins" (Acts 13:38); "God commendeth His love toward us, in that, while we were yet sinners, Christ died for us" (Rom 5:8); "Herein is love, not that we loved God, but that He loved us" (1 Jn 4:10); "We love Him, because He first loved us" (1 Jn 4:19). To this, also, all the prophets had given witness: thus, "I will pardon all their iniquities" (Jer 33:8); "There is forgiveness with Thee, that Thou mayest be feared" (Ps 130:4); "As far as the east is from the west, so far hath He removed our transgressions from us" (Ps 103:12); "I, even I, am He that blotteth out thy transgressions for mine own sake, and will not remember thy sins" (Is 43:25).

Yet it is not merely a question of motives and stimulants that is indicated in all this. It is one of release from bondage; it is the dissolution of the law's curse. Under law and its curse, a man works for self and Satan; under grace he works for God. It is forgiveness that sets a man working for God. He does not work in order to be forgiven, but because he has been forgiven, and the consciousness of his sin being pardoned makes him long more for its entire removal than ever he did before.

An unforgiven man cannot work. He has not the will, nor the power, nor the liberty. He is in chains. Israel in Egypt could not serve Jehovah. "Let My people go, that they may serve Me," was God's message to Pharaoh (Ex 8:1): first liberty, then service.

A forgiven man is the true worker, the true lawkeeper. He can, he will, he must work for God. He has come into contact with that part of God's character which warms his cold heart. Forgiving love constrains him. He cannot but work for Him who has removed his sins from him as far as the east is from the west. Forgiveness has made him a free man, and given him a new and most loving Master. Forgiveness, received freely from the God and Father of our Lord Jesus Christ, acts as a spring, an impulse, a stimulus of divine potency. It is more irresistible than law, or terror, or threat. A half forgiveness, an uncertain justification, a changeable peace, may lead to careless living and more careless working, may slacken the energy and freeze up the springs of action (for it shuts out that aspect of God's character which gladdens and quickens); but a complete and assured pardon can have no such effect. This is "the truth which is after godliness" (Ti 1:1). Its tendencies toward holiness and consistency of life are marvelous in their power and certainty. Irrepressible we may truly call the momentum which owes its intensity to the entireness and sureness of the pardon, a momentum on which some, in their ignorance of Scripture, as well as of the true deep springs of human action, would fasten their drag of doubt and uncertainty, lest what they call the interests of morality should be compromised. As if men could be made unholy by knowing certainly with what a holy love they have been freely loved, or made holy by being kept in suspense as to their own personal reconciliation with God! As if pardon, doled out in crumbs or drops (and even these so cautiously held out, or rather held back, that a man can hardly ever be sure of having them) were more likely to be fruitful in good works than a pardon given at once, and given in such a way as to be sure even to the chief of sinners—a pardon worthy, both in its greatness and its freeness, of the boundless generosity of God!

It would be well for many if they would study Mr. Robert Haldane's *Exposition of the Epistle to the Romans*, especially the second volume. It is a noble protest against the meager teaching of many so-called Protestants on the subject of justification by faith. Its faithful condemnation of the false, and bold vindication of the true may be reckoned too "decided," perhaps "extreme," by "advanced" theologians, but the church of God, in these days of diluted doctrine, will be thankful for such an assertion of Reformation theology. His strong point is his elucidation of the apostle's statements as to the believer's being "dead to sin," which he shows to have "no reference to the character of believers, but exclusively to their state before God, as the ground on which their sanctification is secured" (vol. 2, p. 22). To be "dead to sin" is a judicial or legal, not a moral figure. It refers to our release from condemnation, our righteous disjunction from the claim and curse of law. This, instead of giving license to sin, is the beginning and root of holiness.

5

The Cross and Its Power

Before I can live a Christian life, I must be a Christian. Am I such? I ought to know this. Do I know it, and in knowing it, know whose I am and whom I serve? Or is my title to the name still questionable, still a matter of anxious debate and search?

If I am to live as a son of God, I must be a son, and I must know it. Otherwise my life will be an artificial imitation, a piece of barren mechanism, performing certain excellent movements, but destitute of vital heat and force. Here many fail. They try to live like sons in order to make themselves sons, forgetting God's simple plan for attaining sonship at once, "As many as received Him, to them gave He power to become the sons of God" (Jn 1:12).

The faith of many among us is, after all, but an attempt to believe; their repentance but an attempt to repent; and, in so doing, they only use words which they have learned from others.

It is not the love of holiness that actuates them, but (at best) the love of the love of holiness. It is not the love of God that fills them, but the love of the love of God.

God's description of a Christian man is clear and well-defined. It has about it so little of the vague and wide that one wonders how any mistake should have arisen on this point, and how so many dubious, so many false claims put in.

A Christian is one who "has tasted that the Lord is gracious" (1 Pt 2:3); who has been "begotten again unto a lively hope" (1 Pt 1:3); who has been "quickened together with Christ" (Eph 2:5); made a partaker of Christ (Heb 3:14); a partaker of the divine nature (2 Pt 1:4); who "has been delivered from this present evil world" (Gal 1:4).

Such is God's description of one who has found his way to the cross, and is warranted in taking to himself the Antiochian name of "Christian," or the apostolic name of "saint." Of good about himself, previous to his receiving the record of the free forgiveness, he cannot speak. He remembers nothing loveable that could have recommended him to God, nothing fit that could have qualified him for the divine favor, save that he needed life. All that he can say for himself is that he "has known and believed the love that God hath to us" (1 Jn 4:16); and, in believing, has found that which makes him not merely a happy, but a holy man. He has discovered the fountainhead of a holy life.

Have I then found my way to the cross? If so, I am safe. I have the everlasting life. The first true touch of that cross has secured for me the eternal blessing. I am in the hands of Christ, and none shall pluck me out (Jn 10:28).

The cross makes us whole; not all at once indeed, but it does the work effectually. Before we reached it we were not "whole," but broken and scattered, nay, without a center toward which to gravitate. The cross forms that center and, in doing so, it draws together the disordered fragments of our being; it "unites our heart" (Ps 86:11), producing a wholeness or unity which no object of less powerful attractiveness could accomplish. It is a wholeness or unity which, beginning with the individual, reproduces itself on a larger scale, but with the same center of gravitation, in the church of God.

Of spiritual health, the cross is the source. From it, there goes forth the "virtue" (*dynamis*, the power, Lk 6:19) that heals all maladies, be they slight or deadly. For "by His stripes we are healed" (Is 53:5), and in Him we find "the tree of life," with its healing leaves (Rv 22:2). Golgotha has become Gilead, with its skillful Physician and its "bruised" balm (Jer 8:22; Is 53:5). Old Latimer says well regarding the woman whom Christ cured, "She believed that Christ was such a healthful man that she should be sound as soon as she might touch Him." The "whole head [was] sick, and the whole heart faint" (Is 1:5); but now the sickness is gone, and the vigor comes again to the fainting heart. The look, or rather the Object looked at, has done its work (Is 45:22); the serpent of brass has accomplished that which no earthly medicines could effect. Not to us can it now be said, "Thou hast no healing medicines" (Jer 30:13), for the word of the great Healer is, "I will bring health and cure; yea, I will cure them, and will reveal unto them the abundance of peace and truth" (Jer 33:6). Thus it is by the abundance of that peace and truth, revealed to us in the cross, that our cure is wrought.

The cure is not perfected in an hour. But, as the sight of the cross begins it, so does it complete it at last. The pulses of new health now beat in all our veins. Our whole being recognises the potency of the divine medicine, and our diseases yield to it.

Yes, the cross heals. It possesses the double virtue of killing sin and quickening holiness. It makes all the fruits of the flesh to wither, while it cherishes and ripens the fruit of the Spirit, which is "love, joy, peace, longsuffering, gentleness, goodness, faith, meekness, temperance" (Gal 5:22). By this the hurt of the soul is not "healed slightly," but truly and thoroughly. It acts like the fresh balm of southern air to one whose constitution the frost and damp of the far north had undermined. It gives new tone and energy to our faculties, a new bent and aim to all our purposes, and a new elevation to all our hopes and longings. It gives the death blow to self, it mortifies our members which are upon the earth. It crucifies the flesh with its affections and lusts. Thus, looking continually to the cross, each day, as at the first, we are made sensible of the restoration of our soul's health; evil loosens its hold, while good strengthens and ripens.

It is not merely that we "glory in the cross" (Gal 6:14), but we draw strength from it. It is the place of weakness, for there Christ "was crucified through weakness" (2 Cor 13:4); but it is, notwithstanding, the fountainhead of power to us. For as out of death came forth life, so out of weakness came forth strength. This is strength, not for one thing, but for everything. It is strength for activity or for endurance, for holiness as well as for work. He that would be holy or useful must keep near the cross. The cross is the secret of power, and the pledge of victory. With it we fight and overcome. No weapon can prosper against it, nor enemy prevail. With it we meet the fightings without as well as the fears within. With it we war the good warfare, we wrestle with principalities and powers, we "withstand" and we "stand" (Eph 6:11–13); we fight the good fight, we finish the course, we keep the faith (2 Tm 4:7).

Standing by the cross, we become imitators of the crucified One. We seek to be like Him, men who please not themselves (Rom 15:3); who do the Father's will, counting not our life dear to us who love our neighbors as ourselves, and the brethren as He loved us; who pray for our enemies; who revile not again when reviled; who threaten not when we suffer, but commit ourselves to Him that judges righteously; who live not to ourselves, and who die not to ourselves; who are willing to be of "no reputation," but to "suffer shame for His name," to take the place and name of "servant," nay, to count "the reproach of Christ greater riches than the treasures of Egypt" (Heb 11:26). "Forasmuch, then, as Christ hath suffered for us in the flesh, arm yourselves with the same mind; for he that hath suffered in the flesh hath ceased from sin" (has "died to sin," as in Rom 6:10), "that he no longer should live the rest of his time in the flesh to the lusts of men, but to the will of God" (1 Pt 4:1, 2).

Standing by the cross, we realise the meaning of such a text as this: "Our old man is [was] crucified with Him, that the body of sin might be destroyed, that henceforth we should not serve sin" (Rom 6:6); where the crucifixion of our old man, the destruction of the body of sin, and deliverance from the bondage of sin, are strikingly linked to one another, and linked, all of them, to the cross of Christ. Or we read the meaning of another: "I am [have been] crucified with Christ; nevertheless I live; yet not I, but Christ liveth in me; and the life which I now live in the flesh, I live by the faith of the Son of God, who loved me and gave Himself for me" (Gal 2:20). Here the one Paul (not two Pauls, or two persons), speaks throughout, as completely identified with Christ and His cross. It is not one part of Paul in this clause and another in that; it is the one whole Paul throughout, who is crucified, dies, lives!

Like Isaac, he has been "received from the dead in a figure"; and as Abraham would, after the strange Moriah transaction, look on Isaac as given back from the dead, so would Jehovah reckon and treat this Paul as a risen man! Isaac would be the same Isaac, and yet not the same; so Paul is the same Paul, and yet not the same! He has passed through something which alters his state legally, and his character morally; he is new. Instead of the first Adam, who was of the earth earthy, he has got the last Adam, who is the Lord from heaven, for his guest: "Christ liveth in him"; "I live, yet not I, but Christ liveth in me" (just as he says, "yet not I, but the grace of God in me"); and so he lives the rest of his life on earth, holding fast his connection with the crucified Son of God and His love. Or again, we gather light upon that text: "They that are Christ's have crucified the flesh with the affections and lusts" (Gal 5:24); and that: "God forbid that I should glory, save in the cross of our Lord Jesus Christ, by whom the world is crucified unto me, and I unto the world" (Gal 6:14).

Standing by the cross, we realise the death of the Surety, and discover more truly the meaning of passages such as these: "Ye are dead [ye died], and your life is hid with Christ in God" (Col 3:3); "Ye died with Christ from the rudiments of the world" (Col 2:20); His death (and yours with Him) dissolved your connection with these; "If one died for all, then were all dead [all died]; and He died for all, that they who live should not henceforth live unto themselves, but unto Him who died for them, and rose again" (2 Cor 5:14–15); "To this end Christ both died and rose, and revived, that He might be Lord both of the dead and living" (Rom 14:9).

Romans 6:7–12, "He that is dead [has died] is freed [justified] from sin [i.e., He has paid the penalty]; now, if we be dead with Christ [or since we died with Christ], we believe that we shall also live with Him, knowing that Christ being [having been] raised from the dead dieth no more [He has no second penalty to pay, no second death to undergo, Heb 9:27, 28], death hath no more dominion over Him; for in that He died, He died unto sin once [His death finished His sin-bearing work once for all]; but in that He liveth, He liveth unto God; likewise reckon ye also yourselves to be dead indeed unto sin, but alive unto God, through Jesus Christ our Lord; let not sin therefore reign in your mortal body [even in your body, Rom 12:1], that ye should obey it in the lusts thereof."

There is something peculiarly solemn about these passages. They are very unlike, both in tone and words, the light speech which some indulge in, when speaking of the gospel and its forgiveness. Ah, this is the language of one who has in him the profound consciousness that severance from sin is one of the mightiest, as well as most blessed, things in the universe. He has learned how deliverance from condemnation may be found, and all legal claims against him met. But, more than this, he has learned how the grasp of sin can be unclasped, how its serpent-folds can be unwound, how its impurities can be erased, how he can defy its wiles and defeat its strength—how he can be holy! This is, to him, one of the greatest and most gladdening of discoveries. Forgiveness itself is precious, chiefly as a step to holiness. How any one, after reading statements such as those of the apostle, can speak of sin, or pardon, or holiness without awe, seems difficult to understand. Or, how any one can feel that the forgiveness which the believing man finds at the cross of Christ is a release from the obligation to live a holy life, is no less incomprehensible.

It is true that sin remains in the saint, and it is equally true that this sin does not bring condemnation back to him. But there is a way of stating this which would almost lead to the inference that watchfulness has thus been rendered less necessary; that holiness is not now so great an urgency; that sin is not so terrible as formerly. To tell a sinning saint that no amount of sin can alter the perfect standing before God, into which the blood of Christ brings us, may not be technically or theologically incorrect; but this mode of putting the truth is not that of the Epistle to the Romans or Ephesians; it sounds almost like, "Continue in sin because grace abounds"; and it is not Scriptural language. The apostolic way of putting the point is that of 1 John 1:9: "If we confess our sins, He is faithful and just to forgive us our sins. . . . If any man sin, we have an advocate with the Father, Jesus Christ the righteous" (1 Jn 2:1).

Thus, that which cancels the curse provides the purity. The cross not only pardons, but it purifies. From it, there gushes out the double fountain of peace and holiness. It heals, unites, strengthens, quickens, blesses. It is God's wing under which we are gathered, and "he that dwelleth in the secret place of the Most High shall abide under the shadow of the Almighty" (Ps 91:1).

But we have our cross to bear, and our whole life is to be a bearing of it. It is not Christ's cross that we are to carry; that is too heavy for us, and besides, it has been done once for all. But our cross remains, and much of a Christian life consists in a true, honest, decided bearing of it. Not indeed to be nailed to it, but to take it up and carry it—that is our calling. To each of us a cross is presented when we assume the name of Christ. Strange will it be if we refuse to bear it, counting it too heavy or too sharp, too much associated with reproach and hardship. The Lord's words are very uncompromising: "If any man will come after me, let him deny himself, and take up his cross and follow me" (Mt 16:24). Our refusal to do this may contribute not a little to our ease and reputation here; but it will not add to the weight of glory which the resurrection of the just shall bring to those who have confessed the Master, and borne His shame, and done His work in an evil world.

With the "taking up of the cross daily" (Lk 9:23) our Lord connects the denial of self and the following of Him. He "pleased not Himself"; neither must we, for the servant is not above his master. He did not His own will; neither must we, for the disciple is not above his Lord. If we endure no hardness, but are self-indulgent, self-sparing men, how shall we be followers of Him? If we grudge labor, or sacrifice, or time, or money, or our good name, are we remembering His example? If we shrink from the weight of the cross, or its sharpness, or the roughness of the way along which we have to carry it, are we keeping His word in mind, "Ye shall drink indeed of my cup, and be baptized with the baptism that I am baptized with" (Mt 20:23)?

The cross on which we are crucified with Christ, and the cross which we carry, are different things; yet they both point in one direction, and lead us along one way. They both protest against sin, and summon to holiness. They both "condemn the world," and demand separation from it. They set us upon ground so high and so unearthly, that the questions which some raise as to the expediency of conformity to the world's ways are answered as soon as they are put, and the sophistries of the flesh, pleading in behalf of gaiety and revelry, never for a moment perplex us. The kingdom is in view, the way is plain, the cross is on our shoulders; and shall we turn aside after fashions, frivolities, pleasures, and unreal beauties, even were they all as harmless as men say they are?

It may seem a small thing now to be a lover of pleasure more than a lover of God, but it will be found a fearful thing hereafter, when the Son of Man comes in His glory, and all His holy angels with Him. It may seem a possible thing just now to conjoin both of these, by avoiding all extremes and all thoroughness, either in religion or in worldliness; but in the day of the separation of the real from the unreal, it will be discovered to have been a poor attempt to accomplish an impossibility; a failure—a failure for eternity, a failure as complete as it is disastrous and remediless. Egypt and Canaan cannot coalesce; Babylon and Jerusalem can never be one. These are awful words: "We know that we are of God, and the whole world lieth in wickedness," and surely the Holy Spirit meant what He said when He enjoined, "Love not the world, neither the things that are in the world; if any man love the world, the love of the Father is not in him" (1 Jn 2:15).

The cross, then, makes us decided men. It brings both our hearts and our wills to the side of God. It makes us feel the cowardice, as well as guilt, of indecision, bidding us be bold and stable, "holding faith and a good conscience"; all the more because the wide "liberality" of modern free-thinking has confounded skepticism with candor, and recognises in religious indifference a virtue and a grace. Not to take any side strongly is no evidence of a large soul or a great purpose. It is generally an indication of littleness.

The furrows drawn by a firm hand are strongly and deeply drawn. It is no surface work; soil and subsoil are turned over with a decision which implies that, if the work is worth doing at all, it is worth doing well. The man of true purpose and strong mind handles his plough resolutely, from end to end of the longest furrow, till the whole field be wrought. Thus do men of true will and aim proceed, both in belief and action. Having put their hand to the plough, they do not so much as look back.

The thoughts and purposes of men bear the impress of the mind from which they emerge, as much in their decision as in their general character. As earth's streams are decided in their flow, and owe the measure of their decision to the elevation of the mountain range down whose steeps they pour, so is it with the opinions and actings of men. Decision is no proof of weakness; it is not bigotry, nor intolerance, nor ignorance, though it has sometimes been the emanation of these, and identified with them.

Everything in the Bible is decided—its statements of fact, its revelations of truth, its condemnation of error, its declarations respecting God and man, respecting our present and our future. Its characters are decided men—Abraham, Moses, Joshua, Elijah, Paul. It speaks always with authority, as expecting to be implicitly credited. It assumes our receiving its teaching not doubtfully but certainly; and it leaves us only the alternative of denying its whole authenticity, or of accepting its revelations, without a qualification and without a subterfuge. To excuse ourselves for doubt and indecision, and oscillation of faith, by pointing to differences of creed is to suggest either that Scripture is not infallible, or that it is not intelligible.

The Bible is God's direct revelation to each man into whose hands it comes; and, for the reception of all that it contains, each man is responsible, though all his fellows should reject it. The Judgment Day will decide who is right; meanwhile it is to God and not to man that we are to listen. For the understanding of God's revelation, each one is accountable. If it can be proved that the Bible is so uncertainly written as to render diversity of thought a necessity, or so obscurely expressed as to keep men in ignorance, then, when the day of reckoning comes, the misled man will have opportunity of substantiating his charges against God, and claiming deduction from his penalty, on the plea of the ambiguity of the statute. Meanwhile, we are responsible for decision—decision, in thought and action, on every point which the Holy Spirit has written; and it is not likely that the Spirit of wisdom and love, in writing a Book for us, would write so darkly as to be unintelligible, or should give such an uncertain sound that no man could be sure as to which, out of a score of meanings suggested by man, was the genuine.

6

The Saint and the Law

"God imputeth righteousness without works," says the Holy Spirit, speaking through Paul (Rom 4:6); and he who is in possession of this righteousness is "a blessed man."

This righteousness is at once divine and human, "The righteousness of God" (Rom 1:17); the "righteousness of Him who is our God and Saviour" (2 Pt 1:1); the righteousness of Him whose name is "Jehovah our righteousness" (Jer 23:6). It is "righteousness without the law" (Rom 3:21); yet righteousness which has all along been testified to by "the law and the prophets." It is the "righteousness which is of faith" (i.e., which is got by believing, Rom 10:6), "without the deeds of the law" (Rom 3:28), yet arising out of a fulfilled law. It is the righteousness, not of the Father or of Godhead, but of the Son, the Christ of God, the God-man; of Him who, by His obedient life and death, magnified the law and made it honorable.

Thus, on believing the divine testimony concerning this righteousness, we are no longer "under the law, but under grace" (Rom 6:14); we are "dead to the law by the body [the crucifixion, or crucified body] of Christ"; we are "delivered from the law; that being dead [namely, the law] wherein we were held" (Rom 7:6).

It appears, then, that the gospel does not change the law itself, for it is holy, and just, and good; that grace does not abate the claims, nor relax the penalties of law. The law remains the same perfect code, with all its old breadth about it, and all its eternal claims. For what is the purport of the gospel, what is the significance of grace? Is it perfect obedience on our part to the perfect law? That would be neither gospel nor grace. Is it perfect obedience to a relaxed, a less strict law? That would be the ruin of law on the one hand, and the exaction of an obedience on the other, which no sinner could render. Is it imperfect obedience to an unrelaxed, unmodified law? That would be salvation by sin, not by righteousness. Or, lastly, is it imperfect obedience to a relaxed and imperfect law? That would be the destruction of all government, the dishonor of all law; it would be setting up "the throne of iniquity," and "framing mischief by a law" (Ps 94:20). The demand of the law is perfection. Between everything and nothing the Bible gives us our choice. If we are to be saved by the law, it must be wholly by the law; if not wholly by the law, it must be wholly without the law.

But while it is clear that the law is not changed, and cannot be changed either in itself or in its claims, it is as clear that our relation to the law, and the law's relation to us, is altered upon our believing on Him who is "the end [or fulfilling] of the law, for righteousness to every one that believeth." If, indeed, the effect of Christ's death had been to make what is called "evangelical obedience to a milder law" our justifying righteousness, then there would be a change in the law itself, though not in our relation to it, which would in that case remain the same, only operating on a lower scale of duty. But if the end of Christ's life and death be to substitute His obedience for ours entirely, in the matter of justification, so that His doings meet every thing in law that our doings should have met, then the relationship between us and law is altered; we are placed upon a new footing in regard to it, while it remains unchanged and unrelaxed.

What, then, is this new relationship between us and the law, which faith establishes?

There are some who speak as if in this matter there is the mere breaking up of the old relationship, the cancelling of the old covenant, without the substitution of anything new. They dwell on such texts as these: "Not under the law," "delivered from the law," "without the law," affirming that a believing man has nothing more to do with law at all. They call "imperfect teaching" that which urges obedience to law in the carrying out of a holy life; they brand as bondage the regard to law which those pay, who, studying Moses and the prophets, and especially the psalms of him who had tasted the blessedness of the man to whom the Lord imputes righteousness without works (Ps 32:1), are drinking into the spirit of David, or more truly, into the spirit of the greater than David, the only begotten of the Father, who speaks, in no spirit of bondage, of the laws and statutes and judgments and commandments of the Father.

Our old relationship to law (so long as it continued) made justification by law a necessity. The doing was indispensable to the living, so long as the law's claims over us personally were in force. We strove to obey, in order that we might live; for this is law's arrangement, the legal order of things; and so long as this order remained there was no hope. It was impossible for us to "obey and live"; and as the law could not say to us, "live and obey," it could do nothing for us. Only that which could reverse this order in our case, which could give life in order to obedience, would be of any service to us. This the gospel steps in to do. Not first obedience and then life, but first life and then obedience.

This argues no weakness or imperfection in the law. For if any law could have given life, this law would have done it (Gal 3:21). But law and life, in the case of the sinner, are incompatible. It is the very perfection of the law that makes life impossible under it, unless in the case of entire and ceaseless obedience, without a flaw. "By the law is the knowledge of sin;" and where sin is, law proclaims death, not life. This text, Romans 3:20, does not apply merely to the operation of law upon the sinner's conscience, convincing him of his guilt; it points also to the instruction which law gives us regarding sin all the days of our life. We learn sin and its details from the law; we learn the penalty elsewhere.

So long, then, as the old relationship continued between us and law; or, in the apostle's words, so long as we were "under law," there was nothing but condemnation and an evil conscience, and the fearful looking for of judgment. But with the change of relationship there came pardon and liberty and gladness. "Christ hath redeemed us from the curse of the law, being made a curse for us" (Gal 3:13); and so we are no longer under law, but under grace. The law is the same law, but it has lost its hold of us, its power over us. It cannot cease to challenge perfect obedience from every being under heaven, but to us its threat and terror are gone. It can still say, "Obey," but it cannot now say, "Disobey and perish."

Our new relationship to the law is that of Christ Himself to it. It is that of men who have met all its claims, exhausted its penalties, satisfied its demands, magnified it, and made it honorable. For our faith in God's testimony to Christ's surety obedience has made us one with Him. The relation of the law to Him is its relation to us who believe in His name. His feelings toward the law ought to be our feelings. The law looks on us as it looks on Him; we look on the law as He looks on it. And does not He say, "I delight to do thy will, O my God; yea thy law is within my heart" (Ps 40:8)?

Some speak as if the servant were greater than the Master, and the disciple above his Lord; as if the Lord Jesus honored the law, and His people were to set it aside; as if He fulfilled it for us, that we might not need to fulfill it; as if He kept it, not that we might keep it, but that we might not keep it, but something else in its stead—they know not what.

The plain truth is, we must either keep it or break it. Which of these men ought to do, let those answer who speak of a believer having nothing more to do with law. There is no middle way. If it is not a saint's duty to keep the law, he may break it at pleasure, and go on sinning because grace abounds.

The word *duty* is objected to as inconsistent with the liberty of forgiveness and sonship. Foolish and idle cavil! What is duty? It is the thing which is due by me to God; that line of conduct which I owe to God. And do these objectors mean to say that, because God has redeemed us from the curse of the law, therefore we owe Him nothing, we have no duty now to Him? Has not redemption rather made us doubly debtors? We owe Him more than ever; we owe His holy law more than ever—more honor, more obedience. Duty has been doubled, not cancelled, by our being delivered from the law; and he who says that duty has ceased, because deliverance has come, knows nothing of duty, or law, or deliverance. The greatest of all debtors in the universe is the redeemed man, the man who can say, "The life that I live in the flesh I live by the faith of the Son of God, who loved me, and gave himself for me." What a strange sense of gratitude these men must have who suppose that because love has cancelled the penalties of law, and turned away its wrath, therefore reverence and obedience to that law are no longer due! Is terror, in their estimation, the only foundation of duty; and when love comes in and terror ceases, does duty become a bondage?

"No," they may say; "but there is something higher than duty, there is privilege; it is that for which we contend."

I answer, the privilege of what? Of obeying the law? That they cannot away with; for they say they are no longer under law, but under grace. What privilege, then? Of imitating Christ? May it be so. But how can we imitate Him whose life was one great law-fulfilling, without keeping the law? "What privilege?" again we ask. Of doing the will of God? May it be so. And what is law but the revealed will of God? And has our free forgiveness released us from the privilege of conformity to the revealed will of God?

But what do they mean by thus rejecting the word duty, and contending for that of privilege? Privilege is not something distinct from duty, nor at variance with duty, but it is duty and something more; it is duty influenced by higher motives, duty uncompelled by terror or suspense. In privilege the duty is all there; but there is something superadded, in the shape of motive and relationship, which exalts and ennobles duty. It is my duty to obey government; it is my privilege to obey my parent. But in the latter case is duty gone, because privilege has come in? Or has not the loving relationship between parent and child only intensified the duty, by superadding the privilege, and sweetening the obedience by the mutual love? "The love of Christ constraineth." That is something more than both duty and privilege added.

Let men who look at but one side of a subject say what they will; this is the truth of God, that we are liberated from the law just in order that we may keep the law; we get the "no condemnation," in order that "the righteousness of the law may be fulfilled in us" (Rom 8:4); we are delivered from "the mind of the flesh," which is enmity to God, and not subject to His law, on purpose that we may be subject to His law (Rom 8:7), that we may "delight in the law of God after the inward man" (Rom 7:22); indeed, that we may "with the mind serve the law of God" (Rom 7:25); that we may be "doers of the law" (Jas 4:11). These objectors may speak of obedience to the law as bondage, or of the law itself being abolished to believers; here are the words of the Holy Ghost: the law of God is "holy, just, and good"; that very law which David loved, and in which David's Son delighted—it would be well for such men meekly and lovingly to learn what serving and delighting in it is.

"Do we make void the law by faith? God forbid: yea, we establish the law" (Rom 3:31); that is, we set it on a firmer basis than ever. That law, "holy, and just, and good," thus doubly established, is now for us, not against us. Its aspect toward us is that of friendship and love, and so we have become "the servants of righteousness" (Rom 6:18), "yielding our members servants to righteousness" (Rom 6:19). We are not men delivered from service, but delivered from one kind of service, and by that deliverance introduced into another, "that we should serve in newness of spirit, and not in the oldness of the letter" (Rom 7:6), as "the Lord's freemen," yet Christ's servants (1 Cor 7:22). Thus, obligation, duty, service, and obedience still remain to the believing man, though no longer associated with bondage and terror, but with freedom, and gladness, and love. The law's former bearing on us is altered, and, with that, the nature and spirit of the service are altered, but the service itself remains, and the law which regulates that service is confirmed, not annulled.

Some will tell us that it is not service they object to, but service regulated by law. But will they tell us what it is to regulate service, if not law? Love, they say. This is a pure fallacy. Love is not a rule, but a motive. Love does not tell me what to do; it tells me how to do it. Love constrains me to do the will of the Beloved One; but to know what the will is, I must go elsewhere. The law of our God is the will of the Beloved One, and were that expression of His will withdrawn, love would be utterly in the dark; it would not know what to do. It might say, I love my Master, and I love His service, and I want to do His bidding, but I must know the rules of His house, that I may know how to serve Him. Love without law to guide its impulses would be the parent of will-worship and confusion, as surely as terror and self-righteousness, unless upon the supposition of an inward miraculous illumination, as an equivalent for law. Love goes to the law to learn the divine will, and love delights in the law, as the exponent of that will; and he who says that a believing man has nothing more to do with law, save to shun it as an old enemy, might as well say that he has nothing to do with the will of God. For the divine law and the divine will are substantially one, the former the outward manifestation of the latter. And it is "the will of our Father which is in heaven" that we are to do (Mt 7:21); so proving by loving obedience what is that "good, and acceptable, and perfect will of God" (Rom 12:2). Yes, it is "he that doeth the will of God abideth forever" (1 Jn 2:17); it is to "the will of God" that we are to live (1 Pt 4:2); "made perfect in every good work to do His will" (Heb 13:21); and "fruitfulness in every good work" springs from being "filled with the knowledge of His will" (Col 1:9, 10).

As to the oneness between divine will and divine law, I need only quote the words of Him who came to fulfill the law, "Lo, I come: in the volume of the book it is written of me, I delight to do thy will, O my God: yea, thy law is within my heart" (Ps 40:7, 8; Heb 10:7).

If law be not will, what is it? And if will has not uttered itself in law, in what has it spoken? Truth is the utterance of the divine mind, but law is the utterance of the divine will. When a father teaches his child, we see simply mind meeting mind; but when he commands or gives rules, we see will meeting will. When Parliament publishes reports of proceedings, or the like, there is simply the expression of its mind; when it passes an act, here is the declaration of its will.

I ask attention to this the real meaning of "law," because it is the key to the solution of the question before us. That question is really not so much concerning the law of God as concerning His will; and the theology which would deny the former would set aside the latter. Conformity to the will of God can only be carried out by observance of His law, for we know His will only through His law.

I do not see how a crooked will is to be straightened unless by being brought into contact with "the perfect will of God"; nor do I see how that will is to be brought to bear upon us for the rectification of our will unless by the medium of the revealed law. Will must be brought to bear upon will, the divine upon the human will, and this must be through that part of revelation which embodies will, unless some miraculous power be put forth in us apart altogether from the truth of God; and he who affirms this may also affirm that peace is to be dropped into us apart from the gospel of peace. The divine volition, embodied in a force or power which we call gravitation, rules each motion of the unconscious planets, and this same divine volition or will, embodied in intelligible law, is that which regulates the movements of our conscious wills, straightening them and keeping them straight, though without wrong done to their nature, or violation of their true freedom.

Should it be said that will and law are now embodied in Christ; and that it is to this model that we are to look, I ask: What do we see in Christ? The fulfiller of the law. He is the embodiment and perfection of law-fulfilling. We cannot look at Him without seeing the perfect law. God has given us these two things in these last days, the law and the living model; but was the living model meant to supersede the law? Was it not to illustrate and enforce it? We see the law now, not merely in the statute-book, but in the person of the King Himself. But is the statute-book thereby annihilated, and its statutes made void? Were Christ's expositions of the law, in the fifth, sixth, and seventh chapters of Matthew, intended to overrule or abrogate the law itself? No; but to show its breadth and purity. And when He thus expounded the law, did He say to His disciples, "But you have nothing to do with this law; it is set aside for all that shall believe in my name"? Did He not liken to a wise man every one who should hear these sayings of His and do them (Mt 7:24); indeed, did He not say, "Think not that I am come to destroy the law, or the prophets. I am not come to destroy, but to fulfill. . . . Whosoever therefore shall break one of these least commandments, and shall teach men so, he shall be called least in the kingdom of heaven; but whosoever shall do and teach them, the same shall be called great in the kingdom of heaven" (Mt 5:17–19)? Now one would think that this should settle the question. For the Lord is speaking of the law and its commandments, lesser and greater, and He is speaking of it as binding on them who are heirs of the kingdom of heaven.

Should it be said that it is only exemption from obligation to the moral law or Ten Commandments that is pleaded for, and not the law or will of God in general, I answer, the Ten Commandments are the summary or synopsis of God's will as to the regulation of man's life; and every other part of the Bible is in harmony with this moral law.

Besides, the Ten Commandments were for redeemed Israel. The Sinaitic code began with redemption, "I am the LORD thy God which brought thee out of the land of Egypt, and out of the house of bondage" (Ex 20:2; Dt 5:6). Israel was to keep them because they were redeemed; "the LORD thy God redeemed thee, therefore I command thee this day" (Dt 15:15). Redemption forms a new obligation to law-keeping, as well as puts us in a position for it. And was it not to Sinai and its burnings that the apostle referred when he said, "We receiving a kingdom which cannot be moved, let us have grace, whereby we may serve God acceptably with reverence and godly fear, for our God is a consuming fire" (Heb 12:28–29)? Some would, perhaps, call this legality and bondage, a motive unfit to be addressed to a saint.

If the objection is to the use of the word "law" or "commandment," as implying bondage, I answer, obedience to law is true liberty; perfect obedience to perfect commandments is perfect liberty. And there must be some dislike of the law's strictness where this dislike of obligation to it is felt; indeed, there must be ignorance of gospel, as well as law, in such a case, ignorance of that very redemption from the curse of the law for which the objectors profess such zeal, ignorance of the complete "righteousness without the law" which we have in Christ. I am persuaded of this, that where there is this shrinking from the application of the law as our rule of life, there is a shrinking from perfect conformity to the will of God; nay, more, there is unbelief in the gospel, the want of a full consciousness of the perfect forgiveness which the belief of that gospel brings; for were there this full consciousness of pardon, there would be no dread of law, no shrinking from Sinai's thunders, no wish to be exempted from the broadest application of Sinai's statutes. In all Antinomianism, whether practical or theological, there is some mistake both as to law and gospel.

But why object to such words as "law," and "commandment," and "obedience"? Does not the apostle speak of "the law of the Spirit of life"? Does he not say, "This is His commandment, that we should believe on the name of His Son Jesus Christ" (1 Jn 3:23)? Is not "the new commandment" said to be only a repetition of "the old commandment which we have heard from the beginning" (1 Jn 2:7)? Does he not speak of "obedience unto righteousness" (Rom 6:16), and of "obedience to the faith" (Rom 1:5)?

When the apostle is exhorting Christians in Romans 12 and 13, is he not giving precepts and laws? Indeed, does he not found his exhortations on the Ten Commandments? "For this, Thou shalt not kill, Thou shalt not steal, Thou shalt not covet; and if there be any other commandment, it is briefly comprehended in this saying, namely, Thou shalt love thy neighbor as thyself. Love worketh no ill to his neighbor, therefore love is the fulfilling of the law" (Rom 13:9, 10). The Ten Commandments are here presented as our guide and rule, which guide and rule love enables us to follow; for the apostle does not say "love is an exemption from the law, or love is the abrogation of the law," but "love is the fulfilling of the law." Love does not supersede law, nor release us from obedience to it; it enables us to obey. Love does not make stealing or coveting, or any such breach of law, no sin in a Christian, which would seem to be the meaning which some attach to this passage; but it so penetrates and so constrains us, that, not reluctantly or through fear, but right joyfully, we act toward our neighbor in all things, great and small, as the law bids us do. Yes, Christ "hath redeemed us from the curse of the law," but certainly not from the law itself; for that would be to redeem us from a divine rule and guide; it would be to redeem us from that which is "holy and just and good."

In other Epistles the same reference occurs to the Ten Commandments, as the basis of a true and righteous life. Thus, in speaking of the family relationship, the apostle introduces the moral law as the foundation of obedience, "Children, obey your parents in the Lord: for this is right. Honor thy father and mother, which is the first commandment with promise; that it may be well with thee, and thou mayest live long on the earth" (Eph 6:1–3), where, writing to those who are in the Lord, and not Jews, but Gentiles, he demands obedience and honor, in the name of the fifth commandment. Yet surely, if any duty might have been left to the impulses of Christian love, without reference to law, it would be that of a believing child to its parent. Was the apostle then a legalist when he referred the Ephesians to the moral law as a rule of life? Did he not know that they were "not under the law, but under grace"?

In the Epistle of James we find similar appeals to the moral law as the rule of Christian life. That he is speaking of the Ten Commandments is evident, for he quotes two of them (2:11) as specimens of what he calls the law. This law he bids his Christian brethren "look into" (1:25), "continue in" (1:25), "fulfill" (2:8), "keep" (2:10), be "doers" of (4:11). And this law he calls "the law of liberty" (2:12); indeed, "the perfect law of liberty" (1:25), carrying us back to the psalmist's experience, "I will walk at liberty, for I seek thy precepts" (Ps 119:45); for law is bondage only to the unforgiven; all true obedience is liberty, and all true liberty consists in obedience to law. This law, moreover, the apostle so delights in that he calls it "the royal law" (2:8), the "perfect law" (1:25), pronouncing those blessed who are "not forgetful hearers, but doers of the work" (1:25). Had this apostle forgotten that we were "not under the law, but under grace"? But he was writing to Jews, some say. Yes, but to believing Jews, just as Paul was when writing to "the Hebrews," and when writing to "the Romans" also (Rom 2:17–29). And do men mean to say that there is one gospel for the Jew and another for the Gentile; that the Jew is still "under the law, and not under grace; and that in Christ Jesus all nations of men are not entirely one" (Eph 2:14–22; 1 Cor 12:12, 13; Gal 3:28)?

If the objection to the believer's use of the law be of any weight, it must apply to everything in the form of precept; for the reasons given against our having anything to do with the moral law are founded upon its preceptive or commanding character. The law, in itself, is admitted to be good, and breaches of it are sin, as when a man steals or lies; but then, the form in which it comes, of *do* or *do not*, makes it quite unsuitable for a redeemed man! Had it merely said, "stealing is wrong," it might have been suitable enough; but when it issues its precept, "Thou shalt not steal," it becomes unmeet; and one who is "not under the law, but under grace," must close his ears against it, as an intruder and a tyrant!

Of angels this is said to be the highest felicity, that "they do His commandments, hearkening unto the voice of His word" (Ps 103:20); just as of those from whom the Lord has "removed transgression as far as the east is from the west," it is said that "they remember His commandments to do them" (Ps 103:12, 18). But if this theory of the total disjunction of the law from believers be true, then angels must be in bondage, and they also to whom Paul refers as specimens of the blessed men whose transgressions are forgiven by the imputation of "righteousness without works" (Rom 4:6). To unforgiven men, law is bondage; but is it so to the forgiven? Do pardoned men hate or love it? Do they dread it or delight in it? Do they disobey it or obey it? Do they dismiss it from their thoughts and consciences, or do they make it their "meditation all the day"? Yet there are men who speak of law as abrogated to a believer, who look with no favor on those who listen to it but pity them as ill-taught, ill-informed men, who, if in Christ at all, are only Christians of the lowest grade, the least in the kingdom of heaven.

And this is said to be the proper result of a believed gospel! This is called an essential part of higher Christianity; and is reckoned indispensable to the right appreciation of a saint's standing before God. The realising of it is a proof of true spirituality, and the denial of it an evidence of imperfect knowledge and a cramped theology!

We can find no such spirituality, no such Christianity in the Bible. This is license, not liberty; it is freedom to sin, not freedom from sin. It may be spiritual sentimentalism, but it is not spirituality. It is sickly religionism, which, while professing a higher standard than mere law, is departing from that healthy and authentic conformity to the will of God which results from the love and study of His statutes. It is framing a new and human standard, in supplement, if not in contradiction, of the old and the divine.

"Not without law to God," says the apostle; indeed, "under the law to Christ" (1 Cor 9:21), and yet he understood well enough what it is to be "not under the law, but under grace."

This dislike of the law as a rule of life, and a guide to our knowledge, both of what is right and what is wrong, bodes nothing good. It bears no resemblance to the apostle's delight in the law of God after the inner man, but looks like dread of its purity and searching light. Nay, it looks more like the spirit of antichrist than of Christ: the spirit of him whose characteristic is lawlessness (*anomia*, "without law") than that of Him who, as the obedient Son, ever did the Father's will, in accordance with the holy law. "I delight to do thy will, O my God: yea, thy law is within my heart" (Ps 40:8). It is granted that "the law worketh wrath" (Rom 4:15), and yet that to a believing man legal threats of condemnation have no terror. It is granted that, in the matter of forgiveness and acceptance, law is to him nothing save as seen fulfilled in his Surety.

That law has no claim upon him which should break his peace, or trouble his conscience, or bring him into bondage; that law can only touch him and deal with him in the person of his Substitute; that the righteousness in which he stands before God is a "righteousness without the law," and "without the deeds of the law"; that the sin which still remains in him does not give the law any hold over him, or any right to enforce its old claims or threats. It is granted that it is in grace alone that he stands, and rejoices in hope of the glory of God, in a condition at all times to take up the challenge, "Who shall lay anything to the charge of God's elect?" "Who is he that condemneth?" But admitting fully all of this, we ask: What is there in this to disjoin him from the law, or exempt him from obedience to it? Are not all these things done to him for the purpose of setting him in a position wherein he may love and keep the blessed law which Jesus kept? And should he not feel and cry, as did the redeemed men of other days, "Oh, that my ways were directed to keep thy statutes"? (Ps 119:5); "Oh, let me not wander from thy commandments" (v. 10); "I have rejoiced in the way of thy testimonies" (v. 14); "my soul breaketh for the longing that it hath unto thy judgments" (v. 20); "make me to understand the way of thy precepts" (v. 27); "I will run the way of thy commandments, when thou shalt enlarge my heart" (v. 32). Psalms 19 and 119 must be very uncomfortable reading to those who think that a saint has nothing to do with the law. Will it be said that such legal Psalms were only for Old Testament saints?

Should any one say that it is not to service, but to bondage, they object, I answer, no one contends for bondage. It is in the spirit of adoption and filial love that we obey the law, even as the Son of God obeyed it. But it is somewhat remarkable that the word which the apostle uses, in reference to his connection with law, is not that for priestly service or ministration, but for menial offices; "that we should serve [*douleuō*, be a slave] in newness of spirit" (Rom 7:6); "with the mind I myself serve the law of God" (Rom 7:25); "yield your members servants to righteousness" (Rom 6:19); so that, as the strictest conformity to the law was that in which he delighted, so it is that in which he calls on us to delight.

When he speaks of not being "under the law," but "delivered from the law," his meaning is so obvious that it is somewhat difficult to misunderstand him. His whole argument is to show how the law affected a sinner's standing before God, either in condemning or in justifying. He shows that it cannot do the latter, but only the former; and that, for justification, we must go to something else than law; for "by the deeds of the law shall no flesh be justified." In everything relating to our justification, everything connected with pardon or the giving of a "good conscience," we are not under law. But does this release us from conformity to the law? Does this make it less a duty to walk according to its precepts, or make our breaches of law no longer sin? Does our being, in this sense, "delivered from the law" cancel the necessity of loving God and man? The summing up of the law is, "Thou shalt love the Lord thy God with all thy heart, and thy neighbor as thyself." Is a saint not under obligation so to love? Would the fulfillment of this be bondage, and inconsistent with the spirit of adoption? Is liberty claimed for a Christian either to love or not to love, as he pleases? If he does not love, is he not sinning? Or does his not being under law, but under grace, make the want of love no crime? Is obedience a matter of option, not of obligation? If it is answered, "No; we will love God with all our heart, but not because the law enjoins";

I answer, this looks very like the spirit of a froward child, who says to a parent, I will do such and such a thing because I please, but not because you bid me.

As the common objections to the observance of the Sabbath take for granted that that day is a curse and not a blessing—bondage, not liberty—so the usual objections to the keeping of the law assume that it is in itself an evil, not a good—an enemy, and not a friend.

Say what men will, obedience to law is liberty, compliance with law is harmony, not discord. The force of law does not need always to be felt, but its object, whether felt or unfelt, is to keep everything in its proper place, and moving in its proper course; so that one man's liberty may not interfere with another man's, but each have the greatest amount of actual freedom which creaturehood is capable of, without harm to itself or others. Law does not interfere with true liberty, but only with that which is untrue, promoting and directing the former, discouraging only the latter.

As with the orbs of heaven, so with us. Obedience to their ordered courses is not simply a necessity of their being, but of their liberty. Let them snap their cords, and choose for themselves the unfettered range of space; then not only is order gone, and harmony gone, and beauty gone, but liberty is gone; for that which keeps them in freedom is obedience to the forces of their constitution, and non-departure from their appointed orbits. Disobedience to these, departure from these, would bring about immediate collision of star with star, the stoppage of their happy motions, the extinction of their joyful light, havoc and death, star heaped on star in universal wreck.

7

The Saint and the Seventh Chapter of Romans

I do not see how anyone with a right insight into the apostle's argument, without a theory to prop up, or with any personal consciousness of spiritual conflict, could have thought of referring this chapter to a believer's unregenerate condition, or to his transition state while groping his way to rest.

It furnishes a key to an experience which would otherwise have seemed inexplicable, the solution of perplexities which, without it, would have been a stumbling block and a mystery. It is God's recognition of the saint's inner conflict as an indispensable process of discipline, as a development of the contrast between light and darkness, as an exhibition of the way in which God is glorified in the infirmities of His saints, and in their contests with the powers of evil. Strike out that chapter, and the existence of sin in a soul after conversion is unexplained. It accounts for the inner warfare of the forgiven man, and gives the apostle's experience as a specimen of the conflict.

The previous chapters show the man forgiven, justified, dead, and risen with Christ. Is not sin extirpated, then? The seventh chapter answers, "No." It no longer reigns, but it fights. It does not, indeed, bring back condemnation or bondage or doubt, but it stirs up strife, strife which the completeness of the justification does not hinder, and which the saint's progress in holiness does not arrest, but rather aggravates, so that at times there seems to be retrogression, not advancement in the spiritual life.

"I delight in the law of God after the inner man," are the words, not of an inquirer, or doubter, or semi-regenerate man, but of one who had learned to say, with saints of other days, "O, how love I Thy law" (Ps 119:97), indeed with Messiah Himself, "I delight to do Thy will, O My God: yea, Thy law is within My heart" (Ps 40:8).

"With the mind I myself serve the law of God" is the language of one to whom obedience had become blessedness, and who was not only looking into the perfect law of liberty, but continuing therein (Jas 1:25), in whose estimation serving righteousness (Rom 6:18), serving God (Rom 6:22), serving the Lord, and serving the law of God, were equivalents. But then he who thus speaks, this very Paul, who had died and risen with Christ, who had been in the third heaven, adds, "I see another law in my members, warring against the law of my mind, and bringing me into captivity to the law of sin, which is in my members. O wretched man that I am! Who shall deliver me from the body of this death? . . . So then with the mind I myself serve the law of God; but with the flesh the law of sin." This is not the language of an unregenerate or half-regenerate man. When, however, he adds, "I am carnal, sold under sin," is it really Paul, the new creature in Christ, that he is describing? It is; and they who think it impossible for a saint to speak thus, must know little of sin, and less of themselves. A right apprehension of sin, of one sin or fragment of a sin (if such a thing there be), would produce the oppressive sensation here described by the apostle—a sensation which twenty or thirty years' progress would rather intensify than weaken. They are far mistaken in their estimate of evil who think that it is the multitude of sins that gives rise to the bitter outcry, "I am carnal." One sin left behind would produce the feeling here expressed. But where is the saint whose sins are reduced to one? Who can say, "I need the blood less and the Spirit less than I did twenty years ago"?

It is to be feared that some are carrying out their idea of "no condemnation," of resurrection with Christ, and of the perfection of the new man, to such an extreme as to leave no room for conflict after conversion. They do not see that while conversion calms one kind of storm, it raises another, which is to be lifelong. To such persons, this seventh chapter of Romans is as great a vexation as is the ninth chapter to the deniers of divine sovereignty: both are conscious that their theology would be more manageable without the explanations and modifications which these chapters force upon them.

They seem to teach that the regenerate man is made up of two persons, two individuals—the old man and the new man, constituting two separate and independent beings, an angel and a devil linked together—the old man unchangeably evil, the new perfect and impeccable. In this case, one is disposed to ask:

1. Who is responsible for sin committed? Not the new man, for he is "perfect," and unless he either sins himself, or helps the old man to sin, he cannot be accountable for the evil done. A good man and a bad one, shut up in one prison, would not agree; but the former, however uncomfortable, would not feel responsible for the sins of the latter. Like David, he might mourn that he dwelt in Meshech, or like Lot, he might vex his righteous soul with the deeds done around him, but he would not take guilt to himself because of his neighbour's misdeeds. It is the old man alone, then, that is the sinner!

2. Who gets the pardon? Is it the old man or the new? Not the new, for he is perfect; and it will hardly be affirmed that it is he who gets pardon for the sins of the old man. It must then be the old man that confesses the sin and gets the forgiveness, and is washed in the blood! Or is there no pardon needed, or none possible, in such a case? Are the sins of the old man unpardonable? If not unpardonable, why is he said to be hopelessly bad?

3. What becomes of the old man at death? Is he cast into hell? Or, if not, what becomes of him? Is he annihilated? If he is the sinner, and if his sins are not pardoned, what is to be done with him and with his sins?

4. For whom did Christ die? Not for the new man, seeing he is perfect from his creation. It must, then, have been for the old man, and for him alone, seeing it is he only that sins!

5. Who is it that dies, is buried, rises, and ascends with Christ? Not the old man, surely? He does not rise again, and sit in heavenly places. Not the new man. He does not die, nor is he buried.

6. Who was it that was born again? Not the new man; he did not need that change. Not the old man; he was incapable of it.

7. Who is it that makes progress? Not the old man. He is beyond improvement. Not the new man, for he is perfect. So thus there is no room for "the inner man being renewed day by day." Scripture teaches that the whole man advances, "increases in the knowledge of God," the old element becoming weaker, and the new stronger, and the individual growing in hatred of sin, love to God and Christ, the righteous law, and every holy thing. But how those who insist on the perfection of the new man and the unchangeableness of the old can teach progress, we do not see.

These questions, thus asked and answered, lead us to the simple conclusion that the language of the apostle is figurative. "Not figurative at all," said a friend to us. "There is no figure in the matter. Only a rationalist would say so. Bible words are all real and literal." Real I grant; not always literal. There are figures in Scripture. When the Lord said, "Beware of the leaven of the Pharisees," He used a figure, and His disciples were wrong in accepting His words literally. They were the rationalists. When He said, "Ye must be born again," He used a figure, and Nicodemus was mistaken in construing His language literally. He was the rationalist. The disciples and Nicodemus, by their literalities, turned our Lord's words into foolishness. So do some among us, by their teaching as to the old and new man. If there be no figure, then there must be two bodies, two souls, two spirits, those of the old man and the new; for a man is a being made up of body, soul, and spirit. If there be no figure here, there will be no figure in Ezekiel 36:26, and it must be maintained that God literally takes out one heart and puts in another—takes out a stone and inserts flesh—in which case the old nature disappears entirely and the new reigns alone.

We know that there is conflict in the soul. But this is not between two persons or personalities, or separate individuals, but between two parts of one person. In the case before us, the one person is Paul—once Saul, now Paul. He feels himself responsible for the sins of the old man; he gets the pardon for the old man's sins; for the old man is but another name for a part of his own very self. It was Paul who was born again, who died and rose with Christ. He was "begotten again," not by the insertion of a foreign substance called "the new creature" into him, but by his becoming a new creature. The whole man is converted, puts on Christ, is washed in His blood, and clothed with the righteousness of God—soul, spirit, conscience, intellect, and will. These are not perfected at once, but the transformation begins at regeneration, and though there are two conflicting elements, there is one responsible self or person.

This mysticism as to the old and new man proceeds on a confusion similar to that which mixes up justification and sanctification. The "old man," in the apostle's figure, evidently means sometimes our former legal condition, and at other times our former moral state. In the first sense, the old man is "crucified," "put off" once for all, in believing, when we cease to have "confidence in the flesh" (Phil 3:3). Thus far it is true that it is not amended, but set aside entirely. In the second sense, there is a daily putting off what is old, and putting on what is new. It is like our putting on Christ, which is done once for all at justification, but also gradually, in the process of renewing, so that in one place we read, "Ye . . . have put on Christ" (Gal 3:27), and in another, "Put ye on the Lord Jesus Christ" (Rom 13:14). The mixture of these two things is the chief source of the errors we have been exposing.

This mysticism or confusion is a serious thing. It has been sometimes taught in such a way as to lead men to believe that their peace rested on the perfection or impeccability of the new man. They were taught that the new man could not sin, that all sin came from the old man, whom they had put off, and that therefore they did not need to trouble themselves about sin. No doubt the consciences of some of these misled individuals shrunk from the full application of this antinomianism, but others went on in sin, not so much because grace abounded, as because they were not responsible for the sins indulged in. The new man in them did not commit the sin; it was the old man who did it all, and what better could be expected of one who was totally incorrigible!

Thus the foundations were destroyed; the ground of reconciliation was not the blood of the Sin-bearer, but the new man; the foundation of peace was a perfect self, and not a perfect Christ. Indeed, Christ was made the minister of sin, and all manner of evil was justified, on the plea that the new man could not sin.

This doctrine, as sometimes stated, reads not amiss. It looks plausible, as professing to rest on the very words of Scripture. But it only needs a slight analysis, a little taking to pieces, to show that its effect, if carried out, would be to destroy the feeling of responsibility, to weaken the sense of sin, to blunt the edge of conscience, to shift the foundation of a sinner's peace from Christ to self, to render the blood of sprinkling unnecessary, to hinder personal holiness, and to supersede the work of the Holy Spirit in the soul. For, as to this last, if the doctrine is true, there is no room for the Spirit's operation, any more than for the blood, as He cannot work in the old man, and does not need to work in the new.

That the Christian is not responsible for sin committed against his better will—indeed, that sin in the Christian is not sin at all—has been maintained from Romans 7:17: "It is no more I that do it, but sin that dwelleth in me." In this, however, the apostle is not shaking off responsibility from himself, but explaining a fact, giving the solution of a difficulty. The verse contains one of those peculiar Oriental negatives which the imperfection of human speech renders necessary, in order to bring out the whole of a great but complex truth, which, in less peculiar language, could not be perfectly enunciated. The passage is only one out of several, exhibiting the same apparently contradictory form of assertion. The others are as follows: "I live; yet not I, but Christ liveth in me" (Gal 2:20); "Unto the married I command, yet not I, but the Lord" (1 Cor 7:10); "I laboured . . . , yet not I, but the grace of God which was with me" (1 Cor 15:10); "It is not ye that speak, but the Spirit of your Father which speaketh in you" (Mt 10:20); "Of such an one will I glory, yet of myself I will not glory" (2 Cor 12:5). From these examples, it is plain that the apostle, in Romans 7:17, did not intend to disavow either personality or responsibility or free agency, but simply to affirm the existence in himself of an overmastering element or power of evil, the consciousness of which led to the statement, "I am carnal, sold under sin," and to the exclamation, "O wretched man that I am! who shall deliver me from the body of this death?"

The dislike which some have to consider this chapter as expository of a saint's daily conflict is by no means a safe sign of their religion or their theology. That peace with God through the blood of Christ should be the beginning of warfare seems to us one of the most inevitable conclusions from the gospel, whether of Christ or of Paul. Indeed, it goes farther back than this, to the first promise regarding the seed of the woman and the seed of the serpent, and this warfare, internal no less than external, has filled up the life of every saint from the beginning. Apostolic conflict is but a reproduction of patriarchal. Abel and Stephen, Noah and Peter, Abraham and Paul, move over the same battlefield, for the church is one, her covenant one, her warfare one, her victory and glory one. Each saint has "groaned, being burdened," the groan has deepened as the light increased, and the New Testament fullness of liberty, instead of diminishing, has intensified the conflict. One can imagine David or Elijah perplexed about this unending war. How thankful they would have been for the seventh chapter of Romans, as the clearing up of the mystery! Yet they fought on, as men fight in the twilight or the mist; they finished their course and won their crown. And shall we, in these last days, fling away the key to the mystery which the Holy Spirit has given us by Paul? Or shall we get rid of the mystery by denying the existence of the conflict? Shall we stifle conscience by calling that no sin which is sin? Shall we extenuate trespass because found in a saint? Shall we sit easy under evil, because done by the old man, not the new, by the flesh, and not by the spirit? Shall we nurse our spiritual pride by calling the internal conflict an abnormal and unnecessary phase of Christian life, ascribing it to imperfect teaching, or meager faith, or the retention of the beggarly elements of Jewish bondage?

We may notice here 1 John 3:9: "Whosoever is born of God doth not commit sin." This cannot mean that no man, once born again, ever commits sin; in that case, there is no Christian upon earth. The apostle, in chapter 1:7–8, takes for granted that the Christian does commit sin; indeed, that he dare not say he has no sin without making God a liar, and showing that the truth is not in him. He means to affirm that the being born of God is the only way of deliverance from sin, and that holiness is the true and natural result of being born of God. This kind of affirmation is common: "None of us liveth to himself, and no man dieth to himself" (Rom 14:7); that is, such is the life which might be expected from us. "He is the minister of God to thee for good" (Rom 13:4); that is, he would be, if he fulfilled his office. It is added, "He cannot sin, because he is born of God"; that is, it is totally contrary to his nature to sin. See also the following passages: "A good tree cannot bring forth evil fruit" (Mt 7:18); that is, it is contrary to its nature to do so, though it sometimes does; "As long as they have the bridegroom with them, they cannot fast," (Mk 2:19); that is, it would be incongruous and unnatural. (Compare such passages as the following: Luke 11:7; 14:20; John 7:7; 8:43; 9:4; 12:39; Acts 4:16, 20; 1 Cor 2:14; 10:21; 2 Cor 13:8.) These passages show that "cannot" often means, not that the thing does not or might not occur, but that its occurrence is wholly against the nature of things. "Whoso abideth in Him sinneth not" (1 Jn 3:6); that is, this is the true and only preservation from sin. God's seed remains in us, for we are "born again, not of corruptible seed, but of incorruptible, by the Word of God" (1 Pt 1:23).

8

The True Creed and the True Life

The alphabet of gospel truth is that "Christ died for our sins" (1 Cor 15:3). By this we are saved, obtaining peace with God, and "access . . . into this grace wherein we stand" (Rom 5:2).

But he who thus believes is also made partaker of Christ (Heb 3:14), partaker of the divine nature (2 Pt 1:4), partaker of the heavenly calling (Heb 3:1), partaker of the Holy Ghost (Heb 6:4), partaker of His holiness (Heb 12:10). In the person of his Surety he has risen as well as died; he has ascended to the throne, is seated with Christ in heavenly places (Eph 2:6); his life is hid with Christ in God (Col 3:3). That which he is to be in the day of the Lord's appearing, he is regarded as being now, and is treated by God as such. Faith, in one aspect, bids him look forward to the glory; in another, it bids him look back upon this weary land as if he had already finished his pilgrimage. "Ye are come unto mount Sion, to the city of the living God, the heavenly Jerusalem" (Heb 12:22).

Surely, then, a Christian man is called to be consistent and decided, as well as joyful, not conformed to this world (Rom 12:2), but to that world to come, in which he already dwells by faith. "What manner of person ought [he] to be in all holy conversation and godliness" (2 Pt 3:11).

It has been matter of complaint once and again that some of those who were zealous for these "higher doctrines," as they have been called, were not so careful to "maintain good works," or so attentive to the "minor morals" of Christianity as might have been expected. They were not so large-hearted, not so open-handed, nor so generous, nor so humble, as many whose light was dimmer; also they were supercilious, inclined to despise others as dark and ill-instructed, given to display their consciousness of spiritual superiority in ungentle ways or words.

This will not do. Greater knowledge, lesser love! Higher doctrines, lower morals! Professing to be seated with Christ in heavenly places, yet walking in the flesh, as if proud of their elevation to the right hand of God! Speaking of the perfection of the new man in them, yet exhibiting some of the worst features of the old! Certainly, one who is "risen with Christ" ought to be like the Risen One. He will be expected to be meek and lowly, gentle and loving, simple and frank, kind and obliging, liberal and generous, not easily provoked or affronted, transparent and honest, not selfish, narrow, covetous, conceited, worldly, unwilling to be taught.

Scripture is wonderfully balanced in all its parts; let our study of it be the same, that we may be well-balanced men. The study of the prophetic word must not supersede that of the Proverbs, nor must we search the latter merely to discover the traces of the "higher doctrines" which may be found in that book. We must not overlook the homely, and the little, and the common; we must stoop to the petty moralities, courtesies, and honesties of tamer life, not neglecting those parts of Scripture which treat of these, as vapid or obsolete, but bringing them to bear upon each step of our daily walk, and delighting in them as the wisdom of the God only wise. There is a vitiated literary taste, arising not so much from reading what is bad, as from exclusive study of one class of books, and these perhaps the more exciting. There is also a vitiated spiritual taste, not necessarily growing out of error or the study of unsound books, but arising from favouritism in the reading of Scripture, which shows itself both in the preference of certain parts to others, and in the propensity to search these others only for their references to certain favourite truths. Let the whole soul be fed by the study of the whole Bible, that so there may be no irregularity nor inequality in the growth of its parts and powers. Let us beware of "itching" ears and eyes. True, we must not be "babes," unable to relish strong meat, and "unskilful in the Word of righteousness" (Heb 5:13). But we need to beware of the soarings of an ill-balanced theology and an ill-knit creed. True Christianity is healthy and robust, not soft, nor sickly, nor sentimental; yet, on the other hand, not hard, nor lean, nor ill-favoured, nor ungenial.

"Brethren, be not children in understanding: howbeit, in malice be ye children but in understanding be men" (1 Cor 14:20).

We want not merely a high and full theology, but we want that theology acted out in life, embodied nobly in daily doings, without anything of what the world calls "cant" or "simper."[1] The higher the theology, the higher and the manlier should be the life resulting from it. It should give to the Christian character and bearing a divine erectness and simplicity; true dignity of demeanour, without pride, or stiffness, or coldness; true strength of will, without obstinacy, or caprice, or waywardness. The higher the doctrine is, the more ought it to bring us into contact with the mind of God, which is "the truth," and with the will of

---

1. [I.e., theology that is not empty, whiny, hypocritical, or affected. —Ed.]

God, which is "the law." He who concludes that, because he has reached the region of the "higher doctrines," he may soar above the law, or above creeds, or above churches, or above the petty details of common duty, would need to be on his guard against a blunted conscience, a self-made religion, and a wayward life.

Though "set on high," we "regard the things that are lowly"; we prize the lofty teaching of the Epistles, but we prize no less "the law and the prophets." We listen to the apostolic doctrine, and learn to say, "I am crucified with Christ: nevertheless I live; yet not I, but Christ liveth in me" (Gal 2:20); yet we do not turn away from the apostolic precepts as beneath us: "Put away lying"; "Speak every man truth with his neighbour"; "Let him that stole steal no more"; "Let all bitterness, and wrath, and anger, and clamour, and evil-speaking be put away from you with all malice"; "Uncleanness and covetousness let it not be once named among you, neither filthiness, nor foolish talking, nor jesting"; "Put off all these; anger, wrath, malice, blasphemy, filthy communication"; "Lie not one to another, seeing ye have put off the old man with his deeds." If it seem strange to some to be told that a redeemed and risen man must be a doer of the law, does it not seem still more strange that one entrusted with the ministry should have such minute precepts as these enjoined: "Not given to wine, no striker, not greedy of filthy lucre, not a brawler, not covetous"?

These are the commandments of the Holy Ghost, and they are law just as truly as that which was proclaimed in Horeb amid fire and darkness. And the true question with us (as we have seen) is not whether we are to obey this law or that law, but any law at all. If obedience to apostolic law be not legalism, then neither is obedience to the moral law; and if our oneness with Christ exempts or disjoins us from the moral law, it exempts and disjoins us from all law whatsoever, for everything in the shape of law, or precept, or commandment, contained in Scripture, is from the one Spirit of God, whether in the book of Exodus or the Epistle to the Romans. We know, indeed, that what is merely ritual or ceremonial is gone, being exhausted and put away by Christ; but what is moral and spiritual remains, and must remain for ever; not one jot or tittle of it can fail. What was moral or immoral four thousand years ago is the same still. What was moral or immoral to the Jew is so to the Gentile still. An Old Testament and a New Testament saint rest on the same rock, are washed in the same blood, eat the same spiritual meat, and drink the same spiritual drink (1 Cor 10:3, 4), have put on the same Christ, are doers of the same law, are members of the same body, are heirs of the same crown (Mt 8:11; 21:43; Luke 13:28; Rom 11:18; Heb 11:40; Rv 7:9–15).

"The law is good if a man use it lawfully," says the apostle, but according to some, the only lawful way of using it is not to use it at all. True, "the law is not made for the righteous man" but for "unholy and profane, for murderers . . . , manslayers" (1 Tm 1:9), and as a traveller who keeps the middle of the way never comes into collision with the fences on either side, so a quiet citizen has no need to concern himself about the laws against murder. Man's law does not touch him who keeps it, but him who breaks it; yet it speaks to everyone, it is a guide to everyone, and the principles or moralities of law are wrought into everyone, and wrought the most into those for whom it was "not made"; so that they who never come into collision with it are just those who are unconsciously, yet thoroughly, obeying it.

The higher life, then, is not a life against law, nor a life without law, nor a life above law, but a life like that of the great Law-fulfiller, a life in which the law finds its fullest and most perfect development. It was so in Jesus; it is so in us, in so far as we resemble Him in spirit and in walk. It is a thoroughly conscientious, upright, honourable life. Some, indeed, seem to identify conscientiousness with bondage; but between the two there is no resemblance, save when the conscience is unenlightened, or has become diseased and weak. When the nervous system of the body falls into disorder, then does Satan often (through this inlet) enter the soul, and perplex the conscience, magnifying fancied sin, and palliating real sin, making men mistake a diseased for a tender conscience. But this ought not to lead to disparagement of thorough conscientiousness, in one who has died and risen with Christ; conscientiousness in little things as well as great, in business, in the ordering of our households, in the laying out of our time and our money, in fulfilling engagements, in keeping promises, in discharging duties, in bearing witness for Christ, in nonconformity to the world.

The man who knows that he is risen with Christ, and has set his affection on things above, will be a just, trusty, ingenuous, unselfish, truthful man. He will "add to [his] faith virtue; and to virtue knowledge; and to knowledge temperance; and to temperance patience; and to patience godliness; and to godliness brotherly kindness; and to brotherly kindness charity" (2 Pt 1:5–7). He will seek not to be "barren nor unfruitful." "Whatsoever things are true, whatsoever things are honest, whatsoever things are just, whatsoever things are pure, whatsoever things are lovely, whatsoever things are of good report" (Phil 4:8), these he will think upon and do.

For there is some danger of falling into a soft and effeminate Christianity, under the plea of a lofty and ethereal theology. Christianity was born for endurance; not an exotic, but a hardy plant, braced by the keen wind; not languid, childish, nor cowardly. It walks with firm step and erect frame; it is kindly, but firm; it is gentle, but honest; it is calm, but not facile; obliging, but not imbecile; decided, but not churlish. It does not fear to speak the stern word of condemnation against error, nor to raise its voice against surrounding evils, under the pretext that it is not of this world. It does not shrink from giving honest reproof, lest it come under the charge of displaying an unchristian spirit. It calls sin "sin," on whomsoever it is found, and would rather risk the accusation of being actuated by a bad spirit than not discharge an explicit duty. Let us not misjudge strong words used in honest controversy. Out of the heat a viper may come forth; but we shake it off and feel no harm. The religion of both Old and New Testaments is marked by fervent outspoken testimonies against evil. To speak smooth things in such a case may be sentimentalism, but it is not Christianity. It is a betrayal of the cause of truth and righteousness. If anyone should be frank, manly, honest, cheerful (I do not say blunt or rude, for a Christian must be courteous and polite), it is he who has tasted that the Lord is gracious, and is looking for and hasting unto the coming of the day of God. I know that charity covers a multitude of sins; but it does not call evil good, because a good man has done it; it does not excuse inconsistencies, because the inconsistent brother has a high name and a fervent spirit. Crookedness and worldliness are still crookedness and worldliness, though exhibited in one who seems to have reached no common height of attainment.

I know also that in this world we shall be evil spoken of, and that it is hopeless to attempt to answer every charge. But let us not suffer an accusation to lie upon us, under the pretext that God will take care of our good name, when perhaps the secret reason was that there was some foundation for the evil report against us, and that our good name had better not be brought to a too public test. Let us clear ourselves when the opportunity presents or the occasion demands. It is not wrong to be jealous of our good name, and to answer frankly the fair questionings of friend or foe. It will be time enough to suffer martyrdom when we are actually tied to the stake. It is foolish and feeble to try to become martyrs before the time. Paul met accusations bravely, and would not allow his good to be evil spoken of (Acts 28:17; 2 Cor 8:20, 21; 11:9; 12:18, 19). Our Reformers met their slanderers bravely and, though they could not stay the pen of the defamer, yet furnished materials for vindicating themselves and their cause most amply. There was only One who was dumb as a sheep before her shearers, who answered not a word; and

He was silent because the chastisement of our peace was upon Him, and to be made of "no reputation" was one part of the penalty He was enduring.

Yet let us know when to be silent, as well as when to speak. It is not always right or seemly to answer a fool according to his folly. Let us learn to bear and to forbear, "giving no offence in anything," nor letting "our good be evil spoken of," seeking the things which make for peace, and the things whereby we may edify one another, providing for honest things (2 Cor 8:21, things excellent or beautiful), not only in the sight of God, but also in the sight of men, having a conscience void of offence toward God and towards men (Acts 24:16, 20). These are memorable words: "The kingdom of God is not meat and drink; but righteousness, and peace, and joy in the Holy Ghost. For he that in these things serveth Christ is acceptable to God, and approved of men" (Rom 14:17–18).

With many of us, the Christian life has not gone on to maturity. "Ye did run well; who did hinder you?" (Gal 5:7). It has been a work well begun, but left unfinished; a battle boldly entered on, but only half fought out; a book with but the preface written, no more. Is not thus Christ dishonoured? Is not His gospel thus misrepresented, His cross denied, His words slighted, His example set at nought? Are sunsets such as we have too often witnessed the true endings of the bright dawns which we have welcomed? Must suns go down at noon? Must Ephesus leave her first love, Laodicea grow lukewarm, and Sardis cold? Are issues such as these inevitable and universal? Or shall we not protest against them as failures, perversions, crimes—altogether inexcusable?

If a holy life consisted of one or two noble deeds—some signal specimens of doing or enduring, or suffering—we might account for the failure, and reckon it small dishonour to turn back in such a conflict. But a holy life is made up of a multitude of small things. It is the little things of the hour, and not the great things of the age, that fill up a life like that of Paul and John, like that of Rutherford, or Brainerd, or Martyn. Little words, not eloquent speeches or sermons, little deeds, not miracles, nor battles, nor one great heroic act or mighty martyrdom, make up the true Christian life. The little constant sunbeam, not the lightning, the waters of Siloah "that go softly" in their meek mission of refreshment, not "the waters of the river great and many" rushing down in torrent noise and force, are the true symbols of a holy life. The avoidance of little evils, little sins, little inconsistencies, little weaknesses, little follies, little indiscretions and imprudences, little foibles, little indulgences of self and of the flesh, little acts of indolence or indecision or slovenliness or cowardice, little equivocations or aberrations from high integrity, little touches of shabbiness and meanness, little bits of covetousness and penuriousness, little exhibitions of worldliness and gaiety, little indifferences to the feelings or wishes of others, little outbreaks of temper, or crossness, or selfishness, or vanity—the avoidance of such little things as these goes far to make up at least the negative beauty of a holy life. And then attention to the little duties of the day and hour, in public transactions, or private dealings, or family arrangements; to little words, and looks, and tones; little benevolences, or forbearances, or tendernesses; little self-denials, and self-restraints, and self-forgetfulnesses, little plans of quiet kindness and thoughtful consideration for others; to punctuality, and method, and true aim in the ordering of each day—these are the active developments of a holy life, the rich and divine mosaics of which it is composed. What makes yon green hill so beautiful? Not the outstanding peak or stately elm, but the bright sward which clothes its slopes, composed of innumerable blades of slender grass. It is of small things that a great life is made up; and he who will acknowledge no life as great save that which is built up of great things, will find little in Bible characters to admire or copy.

If we would aim at a holy and useful life, let us learn to

redeem time. "I am large about redeeming time," says Richard Baxter in the Preface to his *Christian Directory*, "because therein the sum of a holy obedient life is included." Yes, let us redeem the time because the days are evil (Eph 5:16; Col 4:5). A wasted life is the result of unredeemed time. Desultory working, impulsive giving, fitful planning, irregular reading, ill-assorted hours, perfunctory or unpunctual execution of business, hurry and bustle, loitering and unreadiness—these, and such like, are the things which take out the whole pith and power from life, which hinder holiness, and which eat like a canker into our moral being, which make success and progress an impossibility, either as regards ourselves or others. There needs not to be routine, but there must be regularity; there ought not to be mechanical stiffness, but there must be order; there may not be haste, but there must be no trifling with our own time or that of others: "Whatsoever thy hand findeth to do, do it with thy might" (Eccl 9:10). If the thing is worth doing at all, it is worth doing well, and in little things as well as great we must show that we are in earnest. There must be no idling, but a girding up of the loins, a running the race with patience, the warring of a good warfare, steadfastness and perseverance, "always abounding in the work of the Lord." The flowers are constant in their growing; the stars are constant in their courses; the rivers are constant in their flowing; they lose no time; so must our life be, not one of fits or starts or random impulses; not one of levity or inconstancy or fickle scheming, but steady and resolute—the life of men who know their earthly mission, and have their eye upon the heavenly goal.

A holy life in man's estimation may be simply a life of benevolence, or of austerity, or of punctual devotion, or of kindly geniality, or noble uprightness, or liberal sympathy with all creeds, all sects, all truths, and all errors. But a holy life in God's estimation, and according to Bible teaching, must be founded upon truth, must begin personally, in conscious peace with

God through the blood of the everlasting covenant, must grow with the increase of truth and deliverance from error, must be maintained by fellowship with God, in Christ Jesus, through the indwelling of the "Spirit of holiness." Error or imperfect truth must hinder holiness. Uncertainty as to our reconciliation with God must cloud us, straiten us, fetter us, and so prevent the true holiness, besides also fostering the false. Fellowship must be preserved unbroken, that the transmission of the heavenly electricity, in all its sanctifying, quickening power, may go on uninterrupted. Nothing must come between: not the world, nor self, nor the flesh, nor vanity, nor idols, nor the love of ease and pleasure.

The Word must be studied in all its fullness. Over its whole length and breadth we must spread ourselves. Above all theologies, creeds, catechisms, books, and hymns, the Word must be meditated on, that we may grow in the knowledge of all its parts, and in assimilation to its models. Our souls must be steeped in it, not in certain favourite parts of it, but in the whole. We must know it, not from the report of others, but from our own experience and vision, or else our life will be but an imitation, our religion secondhand, and therefore second rate. Another cannot breathe the air for us, nor eat for us, nor drink for us. We must do these for ourselves. So no one can do our religion for us, nor infuse into us the life of truth which he may possess. These are not things of proxy or merchandise, or human impartation. Out of the book of God and by the Spirit of God must each one of us be taught, or else we learn in vain. Hence the exceeding danger of human influence or authority. A place of influence in such a case becomes perilous alike to the possessor of the influence and to those over whom that sway is wielded. Even when altogether on the side of truth, its issue may be but an unfruitful formalism, a correct petrifaction, an intelligent orthodoxy; and both they who possess the influence or are under its power ought to be greatly on their guard lest the human supplant the divine, and the fear of God be "taught by the precept of men" (Is 29:13), lest an artificial piety be the result, a mere facsimile religion, without vitality, without comfort, and without influence.

One who has "learned of Christ," who "walks with God," will not be an artificial man, not one playing a part or sustaining a character. He will be thoroughly natural in manners, words, looks, tones, and habits. He will be like that most natural of all creatures, a little child. Christianity becomes repulsive the moment that it is suspected to be fictitious. Religion must be ingenuous. No affectation, nor pedantry, nor conceit, nor set airs, nor what the world calls "whining," can serve the cause of Christ, or give weight to character, or win an adversary of the cross. The "epistles of Christ," to be "known and read of all men," must be transparent and natural. In living for Christ, we must follow Him fully, not copying a copy, but copying Himself; otherwise ours will be an imperfect testimony, a reflected and feeble religion, devoid of ease, and simplicity, and grace, bearing the marks of imitation and art, if not of forgery.

9

Counsels and Warnings

That which among men so frequently takes the name of holiness is very unlike the Bible reality. Whether used in connection with the hardness of a lifeless orthodoxy, or the genialities of a fond idealism, or the smooth regularities of a mechanical devotion, or the religiousness of pictorial superstition, or the austerities of self-righteous mortification, or the sentimentalisms of liberalised theology, or the warm dreams of an earnest pantheism, the words "holy" and "holiness" and "spirituality" have become misnomers or ciphers, as ambiguous in meaning and profane in use as would have been Aaron's ephod upon the shoulders of a priest of Baal. This retention of Bible formulas and a Bible terminology after the expulsion or perversion of Bible meaning is one of the sacrilegious dishonesties of the age, which are so uncomfortably offensive to a straightforward student of the Word.

Holiness may be called spiritual perfection, as righteousness is legal completeness, and both are exhibited in Christ. He is the representation, the illustration, the model. Likeness to Him is holiness. He that is holy is conformed to His image. Every other ideal is vanity. We must learn from the four Gospels what living holiness is, and for a doctrinal exposition of it we must turn to the Epistles. Thus we shall understand both what it is not and what it is.

"Abide in Me," "learn of Me," "follow Me," are the contents and summing-up of the Christian statute book, constituting our true directory and guide in the pursuit of holiness. Here we have:

1. *The life.* From the Prince of life the new life comes to us, even out of His death and tomb, for "we are planted together in the likeness of His death, that we may be also in that of His resurrection" (Rom 6:5); "we are dead (have died), and our life is hid with Christ in God" (Col 3:3). Thus we are "alive unto righteousness"; we live, and yet not we, but Christ in us. We come to Him for life, or rather, first of all, He comes to us with life; we "apprehend Him," or rather, first of all, "we are apprehended of Him"; and the "abiding in Him" is but a continuance of the first act of "coming," a doing of the same thing all our life which we did at first. Thus we live. Thus life increases by a daily influx, and as yesterday's sunshine will not do for today, nor today's for tomorrow, so must there be the constant communication of heavenly life, else there will be immediate relapse into death and darkness. Because He lives, we live, and shall live for ever. His life is ours, and our Christianity must be (like its fountainhead) a thing of vitality, and power, and joy; our life the most genial, earnest, and useful of all lives, "out of us flowing rivers of living water" (Jn 7:38).

2. *The scholarship.* "Learn of Me." His is the school of heaven, the school of light. Here there is all truth and no error. The Tutor is as perfect as He is "meek and lowly." He is at once the teacher and the lesson. With Him is the perfection of training

and discipline and wisdom. There is no flaw, no failure, no incompleteness in the education which He imparts. He teaches to know, to love, to act, to endure, to rejoice, and to be sorrowful, "to be full and to suffer want." The range of scholarship enjoyed by His disciples is only to be measured by His divine stores, His "treasures of wisdom and knowledge." And the end of His instruction and discipline is to make us holy men, conformed to His likeness, and imitators of His heavenly perfection.

3. *The walk.* "Follow Me." It is not merely a life to which we are called, but a walk (a "walking about," as the Greek implies); not a sitting alone; not a private enjoying of religion, but a walk—a walk in which we are visible on all sides, a walk which fixes many eyes upon us, a walk in which we are "made a spectacle" to heaven, earth and hell. It is no motionless resting or retirement from our fellows, but a moving about in the midst of them, a coming into contact with friends and foes, a going to and fro upon the highways and byways of earth. As was the Master so must the servant be. On His way to the cross He looked round and said, "Follow Me" (Jn 12:26); on His way to the throne, after He had passed the cross, He said the same (Jn 21:22). To the cross, then, and to the crown alike, we are to follow Him. It is one way to both.

He then that would be holy must be like Christ, and he that would be like Christ must be "filled with the Spirit"; he that would have in him the mind of Christ must have the same "anointing" as He had, the same indwelling and inworking Spirit, the Spirit of "adoption," of life, faith, truth, liberty, strength, and holy joy. it is through this mighty Quickener that we are quickened; it is through "sanctification of the Spirit" that we are sanctified (2 Th 2:13; 1 Pt 1:2). It is as our Guest that He does His work, not working without dwelling, nor dwelling without working (2 Tm 1:14), not exerting a mere influence, like that of music on the ruffled soul, but coming into us and abiding with us; so that being "filled with His company," as well as pervaded by His power, we are thoroughly "transformed." He does not merely ply us with arguments, nor affect us with "moral suasion," but impresses us with the irresistible touch of His divine hand, and penetrates us with His own vital energy; indeed, He impregnates us with His own purity and life, in spite of desperate resistance and unteachableness and unbelief on our part, all the days of our life.

He that would be like Christ, moreover, must *study* Him. We cannot make ourselves holy by merely trying to be so, any more than we can make ourselves believe and love by simple energy of endeavour. No force can effect this. Men try to be holy, and they fail. They cannot by direct effort work themselves into holiness. They must gaze upon a holy object and so be changed into its likeness "from glory to glory" (2 Cor 3:18). They must have a holy Being for their bosom friend. Companionship with Jesus, like that of John, can alone make us to resemble either the disciple or the Master.

He that would be holy must *steep himself in the Word*, must bask in the sunshine which radiates from each page of revelation. It is through the truth that we are sanctified (Jn 17:17). Exposing our souls constantly to this light, we become more thoroughly "children of the light," and

> Like the stain'd web that whitens in the sun,
> Grow pure by being purely shone upon.

For against evil, divine truth is quick and powerful. It acts like some chemical ingredient that precipitates all impurities, and leaves the water clear. It works like a spell of disenchantment against the evil one, casting him out, and casting him down. It is "the sword of the Spirit," with whose keen edge we cut our way through hostile thousands. It is the rod of Moses, by which we divide the Red Sea, and defeat Amalek, and bring water from the desert rock. What evil, what enemy, within or without, is there that can withstand this unconquered and unconquerable Word? Satan's object at present is to undermine that Word, and to disparage its perfection. Let us the more magnify it, and the more make constant use of it. It is indeed only a fragment of man's language, made up of human letters and syllables, but it is furnished with superhuman virtue. That rod in the hand of Moses, what was it? A piece of common wood. Yet it cut the Red Sea in twain. That serpent on the pole, what was it? A bit of brass. Yet it healed thousands. Why all this? Because that wood and that brass were connected with omnipotence, conductors of the heavenly electricity. So let the Bible be to us the book of all books, for wounding, healing, quickening, strengthening, comforting, and purifying.

Yet, he that would be holy must *fight*. He must war a good warfare (1 Tm 1:18); fight the good fight of faith (1 Tm 6:12), though not with carnal weapons (2 Cor 10:4). He must fight upon his knees, being sober, and watching unto prayer (1 Pt 4:7). He must wrestle with principalities and powers, being strong in the Lord and the power of His might, having put on the whole armour of God, girdle, breastplate, shield, helmet, and sword (Eph 6:13–17). This battle is not to the strong (Eccl 9:11), but to the weak; it is fought in weakness, and the victory is to them that have no might; for in this conflict time and chance do not happen to all; but we count upon victory from the first onset, being made more than conquerors through Him that loved us, and are cheered with the anticipation of the sevenfold reward "to him that overcometh" (Rv 2:7). Though in this our earthly course and combat we have the hostility of devils, we have the ministry of angels in aid (Heb 1:14), as well as the power of the Holy Ghost (Eph 1:13).

He that would be holy must *watch*. "Watch thou in all things" (2 Tm 4:5); "watch ye, stand fast in the faith, quit you like men, be strong" (1 Cor 16:13). Let the sons of night sleep or stumble in the darkness, but let us, who are of the day, be sober, lest temptation overtake us, and we be ensnared in the wiles of the devil, or the seductions of this wanton world. "Blessed is he that watcheth" (Rv 16:15). In watching let us witness a good confession (1 Tm 6:13), not ashamed of Him whose badge we bear; let us run a swift and patient race; "let us lay aside every weight, and the sin [unbelief] which doth so easily beset us" (Heb 12:1), and "follow after righteousness, godliness, faith, love, patience, meekness" (1 Tm 6:11), having our eye upon the coming and the kingdom of our Lord Jesus.

He that would be holy must *feel his responsibility for being so*, both as a member of Christ's body and a partaker of the Holy Ghost. The thought that perfection is not to be reached here ought not to weaken that sense of responsibility, nor lead us to give way to aught that would "grieve the Holy Spirit of God whereby we are sealed unto the day of redemption." The sevenfold fullness of the risen Christ (Rv 2:1), and the sevenfold fullness of the Holy Ghost (Rv 5:6)—these are the church's birthright, and for no mess of pottage is she to sell it; indeed, for the personal possession of that fullness, in so far as vessels such as ours can contain it, each saint is responsible. We are sanctified by the blood (Heb 13:12), that we may be sanctified by the Holy Ghost (1 Cor 6:11), be led by the Spirit (Gal 5:18), be temples of the Holy Ghost, even in our bodies (1 Cor 6:19), walking in the Spirit (Gal 5:16), speaking by the Spirit (1 Cor 12:3), living in the Spirit (Gal 5:25), and having the communion of the Holy Ghost (2 Cor 13:14).

The doctrine of the personality and energy of the Holy Spirit was not more offensive to the cold infidelity of the last century than it is to the more earnest and plausible idealism of the present day. It is set aside as savouring of superstition, and at variance with human liberty and self-power. Energies from beneath or from above are either denied, or recognised only as "principles" or "sensations," or developments of natural law, not connected with personalities in either case. Supernatural personalities are exploded relics of superstition! The thought that there was one perfect and superhuman book, in this world of imperfect literature, used to be cheering; but if modern theories of inspiration be true, this consolation is gone, and the world is left thoroughly disconsolate, without one fragment of the superhuman or the perfect in the midst of it.

The Christian man must not trifle with sin under any pretense; least of all on the plea that he is not "under the law." The apostolic precepts and warnings are quite as explicit as the Mosaic, and much more numerous. He that thinks himself free from the latter will have no difficulty in persuading himself that he may set aside the former; and he who reckons it bondage to listen to the Sinaitic statute, "Thou shalt not kill," will think it equal bondage to hearken to the Pauline commandment: "Be not drunk with wine," or "Owe no man anything," or "Let him that stole steal no more."

As possessors of the Spirit of love, we must be loving, laying aside all malice, and guile, and hypocrisies, and evil-speaking, discharging daily the one debt that is never to be paid (Rom 13:8). For the indwelling Spirit is not idle nor barren, but produces fruit, divine fruit in human hearts, heavenly fruit on earthly soil, fruit which indicates its inner source, and tells of the glorious Guest within; "for the fruit of the Spirit is love, joy, peace, longsuffering, gentleness, goodness, faith, meekness, temperance: against such there is no law" (Gal 5:22–23).

As those whose feet have found the rock, let us be stable, not carried about with every wind of doctrine, not vacillating nor undecided nor compromising. As those who have been "delivered from a present evil world," let us, like the saints of old, be separate from it, standing aloof from its gaieties, as men who have no time for such things, even were they harmless, keeping our raiment undefiled. Let us be suspicious of its foolish talking and jesting, jealous of its light literature, which "eats as doth a canker," vitiating the taste, and enervating the soul. Let us maintain unblunted the edge of our relish for prayer and fellowship with God, as the great preservative against the seductions of the age; for only intimacy with God can keep us from intimacy with the world. Let us not try to combine the novel and the Bible, the closet and the ballroom; nor attempt to serve two masters, to drink two cups (1 Cor 10:21), to worship two gods, to enjoy two religions, to kneel at two altars.

Let us be on our guard against old self in every form, whether it be indolence, or temper, or coldness, or rudeness, or disobligingness, or slovenliness, or shabbiness, or covetousness, or flippancy, or self-conceit, or pride, or cunning, or obstinacy, or sourness, or levity, or foolishness, or love of preeminence. Let us cultivate a tender conscience, avoiding old notions and conceits; yet watching against the commission of little sins, and the omission of little duties; redeeming the time, yet never in a hurry; calm, cheerful, frank, happy, genial, generous, disinterested, thoughtful of others. Seeing we must protest against the world on so many important points, let us try to differ from it as little as possible on things indifferent, always showing love to those we meet with, however irreligious and unlovable, especially avoiding a contemptuous spirit or an air of superiority.

As disciples of Christ, let our discipleship be complete and consistent, our connection with Him exhibiting itself in conformity to His likeness, our life a comprehensive creed, our walk the embodiment of all that is honest, and lovely, and of good report. Christ's truth sanctifies as well as liberates; His wisdom purifies as well as quickens. Let us beware of accepting the liberty without the holiness, the wisdom without the purity, the peace without the zeal and love.

Let us be true men, in the best sense of the word: true to ourselves, true to our new birth and our new name, true to the church of God, true to the indwelling Spirit, true to Christ and to the doctrine concerning Him, true to that book of which He is the sum and the burden. Let us be true to truth, loving it, not because it is pleasant or picturesque or ancient, but because it is true and divine. On it let us feed, with appetite whetted new every day; so shall we add not one, but many cubits to our stature, growing in grace and in the knowledge of our Lord Jesus Christ.

There is such a thing in the church as poverty of blood—hence the blotches that discolour her. For the removal of these, not mere medicine is needed, but a more generous diet. That diet is only to be found in the Word, which is as nourishing (Jer 15:16) as it is healing and purifying to the blood, being truly what old Tyndale calls it, "the word of our soul's health." There is needed, too, the infusion of richer blood, to be brought about by a second Pentecost, in which the existing life will be greatly intensified, and large additions made by conversions of a deeper kind than heretofore. So shall our leanness of faith, of love, of life, of zeal, of joy be efficaciously and abidingly cured. So shall we "come behind in no gift; waiting for the coming of our Lord Jesus Christ" (1 Cor 1:7).

Our spiritual constitution must be braced, not only that we may be strong for work or fight, but that we may be proof against the infection of the times, against the poison with which the god of this world, "the prince of the power of the air," has impregnated our atmosphere. For this we need not only the "strong meat" recommended by the apostle (Heb 5:12–14), but the keen fresh mountain air of trial, vicissitude, and hardship, by means of which we shall be made hardy in constitution and robust in frame, impervious to the contagion around (whether that come from ecclesiastical pictorialism or religious liberalism), impregnable against the assaults of Satan the Pharisee, or Satan the Sadducee. They who have slid into a creed (they know not how), or dreamed themselves into it, or been swept into it by the crowd; they to whom the finding of a creed has been a matter of reading, education, or emotion; they to whom faith has been but the result of an intellectual conflict, not a life and death struggle of conscience, these possess not the true power of resistance. They carry no disinfecting virtue, no error-repelling power about with them. The epidemics of the age tell sorely upon them, and even though they may have taken hold of the truth, it becomes evident that the truth has not taken hold of them. In a time of uncertainty, skepticism, speculation, false progress, we need to recognise the full meaning of the apostolic "we know" (1 Jn 5:13–20), "we believe" (2 Cor 4:13), "we are confident" (2 Cor 5:6), "we are persuaded" (2 Tm 1:12). For that which is divine must be true; that which is revealed must be certain, and that which is thus divinely true and certain must be immortal. Like the results of the exact sciences, it is fixed, not varying with men and ages. That which was true, is true, and shall be true forever. It is the more needful to recognise all this because the ground underneath us has been thoroughly mined and is very largely hollow; a process of skeptical decomposition and disintegration has been going on, the extent of which will soon be manifest when the treacherous crust gives way.[1]

At the same time, let us beware, in the details of personal religion, merely of repeating the past, or getting up an imitation of religion. The genuine in life does not thus repeat itself; nor does it need to do so. The living face of man is of a certain type; yet each face varies from its fellow. The Holy Spirit's work is not to form mere statues. He produces life, and life is always varied. It is death that repeats itself. As silence is always the same, so is it with death. The presence of life is the security against tame monotony. The larger the infusion of life, the greater the diversity, not of gifts merely, but of beauty, and fruit, and power. Let

---

1. "The thoughts of men are widened with the process of the suns," says the philosophic poet of the age, and the maxim seems accepted. In so far as the widening thoughts are honest developments of revelation, the maxim will only express the apostolic "going on unto perfection," "increasing in the knowledge of God." In so far as they are the results of disengagement from the trammels of revelation, they will express nothing but the progress of uncontrolled free thinking.

us not then seek the living among the dead, not try to revivify old forms. Let us place ourselves simply in the hands of the quickening Spirit. He will pour into us the fullness of a diversified, fruitful, healthful life. The evil in us is too strong for any power save omnipotence. The resistance of a human will is too powerful for philosophy or logic, or poetry or eloquence. The Holy One alone can make us holy.

Life is not one battle but many. It is made up, too, of defeats as well as victories. Let us not be unduly troubled or grow moody when a battle is lost. There is always time to win another, and such a thing as flight or demoralization should be unknown in the army of the living God. It is the lost battles of the world (like Thermopylae) that have told most on a nation's history. "If God be for us, who can be against us?" "Thou hast girded me with strength unto the battle" (Ps 18:39).

The Christian life is a great thing, one of the greatest things on earth. Made up of daily littles, it is yet in itself not a little thing, but in so far as it is truly lived, whether by poor or rich, by child or full-grown man, is noble throughout—a part of that great whole, in which and by which is to be made known to the principalities and powers in heavenly places the manifold wisdom of God (Eph 3:10).

It does not need to be a long life; a short one may be as true and holy as a long one. A short one is not a failure. John the Baptist had perhaps the shortest ministry in the church, yet it was no failure; it was one of the greatest successes. He was a burning and a shining light. We do not need to say profanely, "Whom the gods love die young," but we may say that it does not need the threescore years and ten to unfold the beauties of holiness.

If the new life were the mere rubbing off the rust of the old, if the sweetening of the Marah well of our corrupt nature were but a common, non-miraculous process, if all goodness be within the easy reach of any earnest man, if a refined literature and a liberalised theology, and the cultivation of the beautiful, and social science, and a wider range of genial recreation, be the cure for all the evil that is in us and in our age—then there has been much ado about trifles, the Bible is an exaggeration, and the gift of the Holy Spirit a superfluous exhibition of power. If sin be but a common scar or wrinkle, to be erased from the soul's surface by a few simple touches, if pardon be a mere figure of speech, meaning God's wide benevolence or good-natured indifference to evil, why tell of wrath, and fire, and judgment, the never-dying worm and the ever-rising smoke? Does God love to torment His creatures by harsh words, or fill their imaginations with images of woe which He does not intend to realise? Or why did the Son of God suffer and weep, and grieve? If error be but a trifle, a foible, a freak at worst, or if it be a display of honest purpose and the inevitable result of free thought, why is the "strong delusion" (literally, "the energy of error") spoken of so awfully, "that they all might be damned who believed not the truth" (2 Th 2:12), and why did the Lord Himself say, once and again, in reference to false doctrine, "which thing I hate"?

As the strongest yet calmest thing in the world is light, so should a Christian life be the strongest and greatest, as well as the calmest and brightest. As the only perfectly straight line is a ray of light, and as the only pure substance is sunshine, so ought our course to be, and so should we seek to shine as lights in the world—reflections of Him who is its light—the one straight, pure thing of earth.

Let us then shine! Stars indeed, not suns; but still stars, not tapers nor meteors. Let us shine! Giving perhaps slender light, but that light certain and pure; enough to say to men "It is night," lest they mistake, but not enough to bring day; enough to guide the seeking or the erring in the true direction, but not enough to illuminate the world. The sun alone can do that. It is the sun that shows us the landscape; stars show but themselves. Let us then show ourselves beyond mistake. The day when all things shall be seen in full warm light is the day of the great sun-rising.

"The night is far spent; the day is at hand." We shall not set nor be clouded; we shall simply lose ourselves in light. And we need not grudge thus losing ourselves, when we call to mind that the splendour in which our light is to be absorbed is that of the everlasting Sun. It is His increasing that is to be our decreasing, and shall we not say, "This my joy therefore is fulfilled."

www.ingramcontent.com/pod-product-compliance
Lightning Source LLC
Chambersburg PA
CBHW021144080526
44588CB00008B/211